Grade 6

Your Turn
Practice Book

Mc Graw Hill Education

www.mheonline.com/readingwonders

Contents

Unit 1 · Changes

Perspectives

Vocabulary 1
Comprehension: Character, Setting, Plot:
Compare and Contrast Graphic Organizer   2
Comprehension and Fluency 3
Comprehension: Compare and
Contrast and Fluency 5
Genre/Literary Element 6
Vocabulary Strategy: Context Clues 7
Phonics: Short Vowels 8
Writing Traits: Organization 9
Write to Sources 10

Alliances

Vocabulary 11
Comprehension: Character, Setting, Plot:
Sequence Graphic Organizer 12
Comprehension and Fluency 13
Comprehension: Character, Setting, Plot:
Sequence and Fluency 15
Genre/Visual Element 16
Vocabulary Strategy: Context Clues 17
Phonics: Long Vowels 18
Writing Traits: Word Choice 19
Write to Sources 20

Environments

Vocabulary 21
Comprehension: Main Idea and
Key Details Graphic Organizer 22
Comprehension and Fluency 23
Comprehension: Main Idea and
Key Details and Fluency 25
Genre/Text Feature 26
Vocabulary Strategy: Greek Roots 27
Word Study: Frequently
Misspelled Words 28
Writing Traits: Ideas 29
Write to Sources 30

Dynamic Earth

Vocabulary 31
Comprehension: Main Idea and
Key Details Graphic Organizer 32
Comprehension and Fluency 33
Comprehension: Main Idea and
Key Details and Fluency 35
Genre/Text Feature 36
Vocabulary Strategy:
Metaphor and Simile 37
Phonics: r-Controlled Vowels 38
Writing Traits: Voice 39
Write to Sources 40

TIME For Kids

Vocabulary 41
Comprehension: Author's Point of View
Graphic Organizer 42
Comprehension and Fluency 43
Comprehension: Author's Point of View
and Fluency 45
Genre/Text Feature 46
Vocabulary Strategy: Root Words 47
Word Study: Compound Words 48
Writing Traits: Sentence Fluency 49
Write to Sources 50

Contents

Unit 2 · Excursions Across Time

Contributions

Vocabulary 51
Comprehension: Problem and
Solution Graphic Organizer 52
Comprehension and Fluency 53
Comprehension: Problem and Solution
and Fluency 55
Genre/Text Feature 56
Vocabulary Strategy: Latin Roots 57
Word Study: Irregular Plurals 58
Writing Traits: Ideas 59
Write to Sources 60

Democracy

Vocabulary 61
Comprehension: Compare and
Contrast Graphic Organizer 62
Comprehension and Fluency 63
Comprehension: Compare and
Contrast and Fluency 65
Genre/Text Feature 66
Vocabulary Strategy:
Greek and Latin Prefixes 67
Word Study: Inflectional Endings 68
Writing Traits: Ideas 69
Write to Sources 70

Ancient Societies

Vocabulary 71
Comprehension: Point of View
Graphic Organizer 72
Comprehension and Fluency 73
Comprehension: Point of View
and Fluency 75
Genre/Literary Element 76
Vocabulary Strategy:
Connotations and Denotations 77
Phonics: Closed Syllables 78
Writing Traits: Organization 79
Write to Sources 80

Influences

Vocabulary 81
Comprehension: Point of View
Graphic Organizer 82
Comprehension and Fluency 83
Comprehension:
Point of View and Fluency 85
Genre/Literary Element 86
Vocabulary Strategy:
Greek and Latin Suffixes 87
Phonics: Open Syllables 88
Writing Traits: Sentence Fluency 89
Write to Sources 90

Past and Present

Vocabulary 91
Comprehension:
Theme Graphic Organizer 92
Comprehension and Fluency 93
Comprehension: Theme and Fluency 94
Genre/Literary Element 95
Literary Elements:
Rhyme Scheme and Meter 96
Vocabulary Strategy: Personification 97
Phonics: Consonant + *le* Syllables 98
Writing Traits: Word Choice 99
Write to Sources 100

Contents

Unit 3 · Accomplishments

Common Ground

Vocabulary 101
Comprehension:
Theme Graphic Organizer 102
Comprehension and Fluency 103
Comprehension: Theme and Fluency 105
Genre/Literary Element 106
Vocabulary Strategy: Context Clues 107
Phonics: Vowel Team Syllables 108
Writing Traits: Sentence Fluency 109
Write to Sources 110

Transformations

Vocabulary 111
Comprehension:
Theme Graphic Organizer 112
Comprehension and Fluency 113
Comprehension: Theme and Fluency 115
Genre/Literary Element 116
Vocabulary Strategy: Paragraph Clues .. 117
Phonics: *r*-controlled Vowel Syllables 118
Writing Traits: Organization 119
Write to Sources 120

Inspiration

Vocabulary 121
Comprehension:
Sequence Graphic Organizer 122
Comprehension and Fluency 123
Comprehension:
Sequence and Fluency 125
Genre/Text Feature 126
Vocabulary Strategy:
Prefixes and Suffixes 127
Word Study:
Frequently Misspelled Words 128
Writing Traits: Ideas 129
Write to Sources 130

Milestones

Vocabulary 131
Comprehension: Cause and Effect
Graphic Organizer 132
Comprehension and Fluency 133
Comprehension: Cause and Effect
and Fluency 135
Genre/Text Feature 136
Vocabulary Strategy: Paragraph Clues .. 137
Word Study: Prefixes 138
Writing Traits: Voice 139
Write to Sources 140

TIME For Kids

Vocabulary 141
Comprehension: Main Idea and
Key Details Graphic Organizer 142
Comprehension and Fluency 143
Comprehension: Main Idea and
Key Details and Fluency 145
Genre/Text Feature 146
Vocabulary Strategy: Synonyms and
Antonyms 147
Word Study: Suffixes *-ion* and *-tion* 148
Writing Traits: Ideas 149
Write to Sources 150

Contents

Unit 4 · Challenges

Changing Environments

Vocabulary 151
Comprehension: Author's Point of View
Graphic Organizer 152
Comprehension and Fluency 153
Comprehension: Author's Point of View
and Fluency 155
Genre/Text Feature 156
Vocabulary Strategy: Paragraph Clues .. 157
Word Study: Suffix *-ion* 158
Writing Traits: Organization 159
Write to Sources 160

Overcoming Challenges

Vocabulary 161
Comprehension: Author's Point of View
Graphic Organizer 162
Comprehension and Fluency 163
Comprehension: Author's Point of View
and Fluency 165
Genre/Text Feature 166
Vocabulary Strategy: Idioms 167
Phonics: Vowel Alternation 168
Writing Traits: Sentence Fluency 169
Write to Sources 170

Standing Tall

Vocabulary 171
Comprehension:
Theme Graphic Organizer 172
Comprehension and Fluency 173
Comprehension: Theme and Fluency 175
Genre/Literary Element 176
Vocabulary Strategy: Homophones 177
Word Study: Prefixes and Suffixes 178
Writing Traits: Ideas 179
Write to Sources 180

Shared Experiences

Vocabulary 181
Comprehension:
Theme Graphic Organizer 182
Comprehension and Fluency 183
Comprehension: Theme and Fluency 185
Genre/Literary Element 186
Vocabulary Strategy: Homographs 187
Word Study: Greek and Latin Prefixes .. 188
Writing Traits: Ideas 189
Write to Sources 190

Taking Responsibility

Vocabulary 191
Comprehension:
Point of View Graphic Organizer 192
Comprehension and Fluency 193
Comprehension:
Point of View and Fluency 194
Genre/Literary Element 195
Literary Elements:
Alliteration and Assonance 196
Vocabulary Strategy:
Figurative Language 197
Phonics: Consonant Alternation 198
Writing Traits: Word Choice 199
Write to Sources 200

Contents

Unit 5 · Discoveries

Myths

Vocabulary 201
Comprehension: Problem and
Solution Graphic Organizer 202
Comprehension and Fluency 203
Comprehension: Problem and
Solution and Fluency 205
Genre/Literary Element 206
Vocabulary Strategy: Word Origins 207
Word Study: Homophones 208
Writing Traits: Sentence Fluency 209
Write to Sources 210

Personal Strength

Vocabulary 211
Comprehension:
Cause and Effect Graphic Organizer 212
Comprehension and Fluency 213
Comprehension:
Cause and Effect and Fluency 215
Genre/Text Feature 216
Vocabulary Strategy:
Adages and Proverbs 217
Word Study:
Words from Around the World 218
Writing Traits: Word Choice 219
Write to Sources 220

Innovations

Vocabulary 221
Comprehension:
Cause and Effect Graphic Organizer 222
Comprehension and Fluency 223
Comprehension:
Cause and Effect and Fluency 225
Genre/Text Feature 226
Vocabulary Strategy: Context Clues 227
Word Study: Latin Roots 228
Writing Traits: Organization 229
Write to Sources 230

Breakthroughs

Vocabulary 231
Comprehension:
Sequence Graphic Organizer 232
Comprehension and Fluency 233
Comprehension:
Sequence and Fluency 235
Genre/Text Feature 236
Vocabulary Strategy: Context Clues 237
Word Study: Greek Roots 238
Writing Traits: Organization 239
Write to Sources 240

TIME For Kids

Vocabulary 241
Comprehension: Author's Point of View
Graphic Organizer 242
Comprehension and Fluency 243
Comprehension: Author's Point of View
and Fluency 245
Genre/Text Feature 246
Vocabulary Strategy:
Connotations and Denotations 247
Word Study: Suffixes -ive, -age, and -ize . 248
Writing Traits: Word Choice 249
Write to Sources 250

Contents

Unit 6 · Taking Action

Resources

Vocabulary 251
Comprehension: Main Idea and
Key Details Graphic Organizer 252
Comprehension and Fluency 253
Comprehension: Main Idea and
Key Details and Fluency 255
Genre/Text Feature 256
Vocabulary Strategy: Latin Roots 257
Word Study: Suffixes *-ible* and *-able* 258
Writing Traits: Sentence Fluency 259
Write to Sources 260

Witnesses

Vocabulary 261
Comprehension: Cause and
Effect Graphic Organizer 262
Comprehension and Fluency 263
Comprehension: Cause and
Effect and Fluency 265
Genre/Text Feature 266
Vocabulary Strategy:
Adages and Proverbs 267
Word Study:
Suffixes *-ance, -ence, -ant,* and *-ent* 268
Writing Traits: Voice 269
Write to Sources 270

Investigations

Vocabulary 271
Comprehension: Main Idea and
Key Details Graphic Organizer 272
Comprehension and Fluency 273
Comprehension: Main Ideas and
Key Details and Fluency 275
Genre/Text Feature 276
Vocabulary Strategy: Context Clues 277
Word Study: Greek Suffixes 278
Writing Traits: Organization 279
Write to Sources 280

Extraordinary Finds

Vocabulary 281
Comprehension:
Sequence Graphic Organizer 282
Comprehension and Fluency 283
Comprehension:
Sequence and Fluency 285
Genre/Text Feature 286
Vocabulary Strategy: Greek Roots 287
Word Study: Absorbed Prefixes 288
Writing Traits: Word Choice 289
Write to Sources 290

Taking a Break

Vocabulary 291
Comprehension:
Theme Graphic Organizer 292
Comprehension and Fluency 293
Comprehension: Theme and Fluency 294
Genre/Literary Element 295
Literary Elements:
Repetition and Imagery 296
Vocabulary Strategy:
Figurative Language 297
Word Study: Words from Mythology 298
Writing Traits: Word Choice 299
Write to Sources 300

Name _____

| consolation | glimmer | indispensable | perception |
| phobic | sarcastic | threshold | heinous |

Use each pair of vocabulary words in a single sentence.

1. perception, heinous

The dark knight brings unique perception
to carry out heinous crimes.

2. sarcastic, phobic

I am not phobic towards those people
she said sarcastically.

3. glimmer, threshold

I saw a glimmer of light come from under
the threshold of the door.

4. consolation, indispensable

your best friends Mother is an indispsable
consolation for your friend.

Name _____

Read the selection. Complete the character, setting, and plot compare-and-contrast graphic organizer.

Characters

Setting

Beginning

↓

Middle

↓

End

Name _____

Read the passage. Use the visualize strategy to help you form mental images as you read.

SMART START

	Normally the cafeteria was so noisy you couldn't hear a tray drop. But
13	now, Alex's footsteps echoed across the huge room. There were a few
25	other scattered students in the cafeteria, all avoiding eye contact with one
37	another. The Dunce Convention, Alex thought, as his backpack landed
47	with a loud thud on the table. He was here after school for his first session
63	in "Smart Start," a program in which students received free tutoring in
75	subjects that were difficult for them. Alex wondered whom the school
86	thought they were fooling with their opposite-name trick. Smart Start
96	meant "Stupid Forever."
99	Alex had been sentenced to Smart Start for math. His parents, already
111	concerned about his grades, were even more agitated because the
121	Statewide Math Aptitude Test was approaching. (Also oppositely-named,
129	Alex thought; in his case, it should be the Inaptitude Test.) Math had
142	always been torture for Alex. For extra humiliation, his little sister had
154	accelerated and was taking the same math subject as he, despite being
166	almost two years younger.
170	Alex unearthed the crumpled registration form and began to fidget with
181	it, a nervous habit of his. Absentmindedly, he folded over the strip with
194	his name on it repeatedly, scoring it until there was a sharp crease. Next,
208	he tore the strip off, bracing the page against the edge of the table. What
223	remained was a nearly perfect square—ideal for one of Alex's favorite
235	pastimes: origami.
237	He began folding one of the common origami patterns, the bird base.
249	Using his thumbnail to form the sharp creases, Alex created a triangle,
261	and added some petal folds. Soon the bird base was complete, and he was
275	partway into making the crane. So absorbed was he, that he didn't hear the
289	footsteps of the person approaching his table.

Name _____

"You must be Alex. I'm Sophia," announced the girl, extending her hand. Startled, Alex quickly shoved his folded paper aside. Sophia continued, "I'm in eighth grade. Tell me a little bit about yourself. What do you like to do?"

"Anything but math!" Alex replied.

"Well, I guess that's why you're here," Sophia said with a laugh. "I used to hate math, too," she offered.

Alex recognized that Sophia was making an effort to put him at ease, so he granted her a quick smile. "What made you start to like it?" he asked politely.

"Believe it or not, I think it was marching band. I realized that counting beats and tracking measures is all about math. Hey, what's that you're hiding?" she teased, tugging at his folded form.

"It's nothing yet, but soon it will be," Alex explained. Quickly, Alex folded and creased, his hands awhirl. "Ta-da—a crane!" he proclaimed, presenting the transformed shape.

"That's awesome," Sophia declared, staring intently at the origami folds. "Do you mind if I take it apart?" Alex shrugged, and Sophia carefully unfolded each step of the crane, leaving a geometric wonder of creases. Sophia looked excited about the wrinkled sheet, and Alex raised his eyebrows.

"Don't you see? What you have here is most of your math curriculum, right in front of you!" She flattened the paper out with the palm of her hand. "Do your first fold," she commanded, and Alex complied. "You began with a square, and created two rectangles. And you have a fraction, too: one half! Fold it again... and, magic, now you have four quarters." Sophia pointed to the top fold. "What fraction does this flap represent?"

"One quarter?" Alex responded.

"Duh! Obviously, right? Get out some more paper, and let's do some geometry!"

If math tutoring was going to be origami, Alex thought, maybe it would be a Smart Start after all.

Name _____

A. Reread the passage and answer the questions.

1. At the beginning of the story, what is Alex doing? What is his
attitude toward the Smart Start group? Why?

Alex's attidude was negative at first. He thought the
group was for stupid people.

2. In the middle of the story, what does Alex start to make? What
is his attitude toward this pastime?

His pastime was making a origami. Doing that calmed
him down and not being nervous.

3. At the end of the story, what is Alex's attitude toward Smart
Start and math?

Alex is at the end thought, maybe it would be
a smart start after all and that proves that he
was like, oh yeah maybe it did help out after all.

4. What similarities and differences do you see between Alex's
attitude at the beginning of the story and at the end?

In the beginning of the text Alex's attitude was
negative and he was mad. At the end he was happy
and was like, maybe this class did help me out

_____

**B. Work with a partner. Read the passage aloud. Pay attention to
expression and phrasing. Stop after one minute. Fill out the chart.**

	Words Read	–	Number of Errors	=	Words Correct Score
First Read		–		=	
Second Read		–		=	

Name _____

The Long Hard Climb

Today is my first day back at school after severely fracturing my femur bone. In all honesty, after three excruciatingly dull weeks at home, I'm ecstatic to be back. Now, I'm looking up at the school's imposing front door, counting the steps: there are ten. Usually I gallop swiftly up the steps every day, but in my perception today, they look like Mount Everest. With my crutches first, good leg second, I ascend.

"Hurry; that's the second bell ringing," Bridget, my best friend, exclaims.

As beads of sweat glimmer across my forehead, I respond, "I'm trying, but I can't exactly catapult myself to the door!"

Answer the questions about the text.

1. List three literary elements that let you know this is realistic fiction.

_____

_____

2. Who is the narrator and what is the narrator's role in the text?

The narrator's role is to make the text funny and interesting by saying "I'm trying but I can't exactly catapult myself to the door!".

3. Give an example of how dialogue is used to show a character's feelings.

Ex. My moms sighed during my parent teacher conferace. this shows my mom is disapointed because of the sigh.

Name _____

Read each passage. Underline the context clues that help you figure out the meaning of the word in bold. Then write the word's meaning on the line.

1. Math had always been torture for Alex. For extra humiliation, his little sister had **accelerated** and was taking the same math subject as he, despite being almost two years younger.

   She gave him courage that he can do it

2. Soon the bird base was complete, and he was partway into making the crane. So **absorbed** was he, that he didn't hear the footsteps of the person approaching his table.

   He was into it that he was not paying attention to other thigs

3. Alex recognized that Sophia was making an effort to put him at ease, so he **granted** her a quick smile. "What made you start to like it?" he asked politely.

   Gave her a thanks by smiling at her.

Use what you know about context clues to explain the following word in a sentence: *pastime.* **Be sure to include context clues that explain the word's meaning.**

   During my pastime I like to think what my schedule the next day will be.

Name _____

A. Read the words in each row and circle the word that has a short vowel sound. Then write the word on the line and underline the letter or letters that stand for the sound.

1. fly   grate   prank   _____

2. scuff   troop   flame   _____

3. joke   jeep   sock   _____

4. shake   brim   bright   _____

5. wait   dent   feast   _____

B. Read each sentence. Find the word with a short vowel sound and write it on the line. Then underline the letter or letters that make the short vowel sound.

6. The ice coating the street was dense. _____

7. The team feels proud of their rank.   _____

8. The truck needs to be repaired.   _____

9. A drill was required for the work.   _____

10. Don't dread the role.   _____

11. Please lock the door.   _____

12. The boys both wore plaid.   _____

Name _____

A. Read the draft model. Use the questions that follow the draft to help you think about ways to give the draft a stronger opening.

Draft Model

I was hiking to the bottom of the Grand Canyon. It was cold and foggy. I could feel the steep cliffs rising sharply above us.

---

1. Why is the narrator at the Grand Canyon?

2. How can you hint at or tell about a problem to make the opening more interesting?

3. Is anyone with the narrator?

4. What does the narrator see and hear while hiking?

B. Now revise the draft by adding details that will grab the reader's attention and make him or her want to learn more about the narrator's hike.

_____

_____

_____

_____

_____

_____

_____

_____

Name _____

The student who wrote the paragraphs below used text evidence from two different sources to respond to the prompt: *Write an email from Gen to one of her friends about visiting New York City to take an art class.*

Hey Kristen,

New York is amazing! It's a bazillion times more fun than "Camp 1890s."

In Wyoming, the days dragged on. It was like time stopped, which it kind of did, because my dad didn't wind his watch, and there weren't any electric clocks. Well, here in New York, time flies! Especially when I'm in art class. The teacher is so cool. For our first project, she told us to think about seeing colors and shapes in everyday scenes. I painted the countryside in Wyoming, because even though it was so BORING, it was actually pretty beautiful there. When I turned the painting in, she asked about my trip. She said that she wished she could go someplace beautiful with no electronics. I didn't tell her about my sneak-texting. :)

After class, I ride the subway to my aunt's apartment. She has an awesome view! I'm looking out the window right now. It's crazy that the moon over this busy city is the same moon looking over Nora and her dad in quiet Wyoming.

See you soon!

Gen

Reread the passage. Follow the directions below.

1. How does Gen feel about New York? **Circle** the statement that shows a strong opening.

2. How did Gen feel about Wyoming? **Underline** supporting details that show how Gen felt about living with no electronics.

3. How does Gen feel about secretly using electronics in Wyoming? **Draw a box** around a sentence that helps the reader infer how Gen feels.

4. **Write** an exclamatory sentence on the line.

_____

Name _____

inflicted	adversity	alliance	confinement
reminisce	retrieved	smuggle	spindly

Finish each sentence using the vocabulary word provided.

1. **(alliance)** In order to defeat the enemy, _____

_____

2. **(inflicted)** The winds from the strong storm _____

_____

3. **(adversity)** We were prepared for the challenge _____

_____

4. **(spindly)** The children wanted to climb _____

_____

5. **(retrieved)** I left my textbook in the living room, _____

_____

6. **(reminisce)** The townspeople liked to _____

_____

7. **(confinement)** After sitting in the small room for a while, _____

_____

8. **(smuggle)** We needed to _____

_____

Name _____

**Read the selection. Complete the character, setting, plot:
sequence graphic organizer.**

Characters
Setting
Problem
Event
Event
Solution

Name _____

Read the passage. Use the visualize strategy to help you form mental pictures as you read.

Appreciation

	It was the first day of school in this Nebraska community, and Hermann
13	had good reason to be nervous. He barely remembered what it felt like to
27	go to school!
30	That had not always been the case. He had been a good student when he
45	lived in New York City. During the 1882 school year, however, his father
58	had become ill. Hermann had to leave school to help his family. When
71	his father finally recuperated enough for Hermann to return to school,
82	his father made an announcement. The family was going to move to the
95	Nebraska prairie to farm as his family had in the old country.
107	This Nebraska life proved to be an extremely hard one, and it kept
120	Hermann and his father busy every day from early in the morning until late
134	at night. First, they had to reinforce the walls of their sod house, which
148	were made from squares cut from the soil, so they wouldn't collapse.
160	Then, in order to keep the wind out, they had to seal the cracks that snaked
176	across the walls, and after that, it was time to plow the fields and tend to
192	the crops. Unfortunately, the attention and effort needed to ensure that
203	they had food on the table left no time for Hermann to attend school.
217	However, when fall arrived in 1884, Hermann's father had made his
228	decision. He wanted Hermann to return to school, because the life of
240	a pioneer farmer was a hard one, and he didn't want his son to have as
256	arduous a life as he had.
262	As Hermann walked the three dusty miles to school, he became more
274	nervous with each step. Would he make new friends? Would he do
286	satisfactorily in school? Back in the city, there had always been someone
298	to talk to, but here there was nobody, and the prairie seemed inhospitable.
311	Walking across the empty landscape, Hermann felt lonely. There was only
322	the occasional sound of whistling wind or howling coyotes to distract him.

Name_____

By the time Hermann reached the one-room schoolhouse, everyone had already gone inside. The last of his confidence evaporated as he walked through the door. "You must be Hermann," a young woman said. "I am your teacher, Miss Peal."

A one-room schoolhouse with teacher and students

Miss Peal pointed to a seat at the far end of the classroom. All eyes were on Hermann as he crossed the floor, and he thought he heard someone stifle a giggle. When he tripped, his classmates couldn't hold it in any longer. They laughed loudly, and by the time Hermann finally sat down, his face was beet red, and he felt humiliated.

"Class, please!" Miss Peal said sharply. Then she smiled and reassured Hermann. "Don't worry, you haven't missed anything," she said comfortingly. "I've just been asking students to read aloud and spell a few words so that I can assign partners."

When it was Hermann's turn to read, he stumbled since it had been a long time since he had been in school. Afterward, he wasn't surprised to be paired with Rosa, a quiet girl approximately three or four years younger.

Before Hermann realized it, it was time for lunch. Hermann seated himself away from the other students and pulled some bread and cheese out of a small sack. Then he noticed Rosa sitting alone. She glanced toward Hermann, looking tentatively. That's when it hit him. "Are you hungry?" Hermann asked Rosa. After she nodded, he said, "Here, I'll share with you."

"And I'll help you in return!" she said. She quickly ate the food Hermann offered, and then she began to rifle through the pages of her spelling book. Finally, she found the page she had been looking for. "Spell the word 'appreciate' and use it in a sentence." Hermann carefully spelled each letter, then he grinned. "I *appreciate* your help," he said.

"So do I," Rosa said, smiling shyly. Finally, Hermann was feeling a little more confident. Even though this had not been a perfect first day, this year had the potential to be a very good year.

Name _____

A. Reread the passage and answer the questions.

1. What is Hermann's problem in the first paragraph?

_____

2. What four different sequence words in paragraphs 10 and 11 help you understand the order of events between Hermann and Rosa during lunch?

_____

3. What is the solution to Hermann's problem? List three events that lead to this solution.

_____

_____

_____

_____

B. Work with a partner. Read the passage aloud. Pay attention to intonation. Stop after one minute. Fill out the chart.

	Words Read	–	Number of Errors	=	Words Correct Score
First Read		–		=	
Second Read		–		=	

Name _____

Women's Rights, 1848

The year was 1848, and Molly Simpson traveled from her home in Baltimore to the Seneca Falls Convention, a women's rights convention in New York. Molly had the honor to present the event's opening remarks and addressed her fellow suffragists: "We are here today because we want the same rights and opportunities as men. We want the vote; we want to be able to go to college and become professionals. We could even become elected officials ourselves!"

The crowd applauded.

Answer the questions about the text.

1. How does the setting let you know this is historical fiction?

   _____

   _____

2. Who is the main character in the text? What is her purpose in the text?

   _____

   _____

3. What are the three main events mentioned in the text and in what order do they occur?

   _____

   _____

4. What illustration could be added to present details of the historical time and support the plot?

   _____

   _____

Name _____

Read each passage. Underline the context clues that help you figure out the meaning of each word in bold. Then write the word's meaning on the line.

1. During the 1882 school year, however, his father had become ill. Hermann had to leave school to help his family. When his father finally **recuperated** enough for Hermann to return to school, his father made an announcement.

   _____

2. He wanted Hermann to return to school, because the life of a pioneer farmer was a hard one, and he didn't want his son to have as **arduous** a life as he had.

   _____

3. Back in the city, there had always been someone to talk to, but here there was nobody, and the prairie seemed **inhospitable**.

   _____

4. All eyes were on Hermann as he crossed the floor, and he thought he heard someone **stifle** a giggle. When he tripped, his classmates couldn't hold it in any longer.

   _____

5. Then he noticed Rosa sitting alone. She glanced toward Hermann, looking **tentatively**.

   _____

Name _____

A. Circle the word with a long vowel sound to complete the sentence. Then write the word on the line.

1. My sister likes to control the television _____.

   channel   remote   picture

2. I love to _____ out of the car window.

   shout   watch   gaze

3. My favorite songs usually include _____.

   guitar   drums   rhyme

4. The team's future is looking _____.

   bleak   drab   better

5. The two armies decided on a _____.

   plan   truce   boundary

B. Read the words in the box below. Then write each word on the line next to the word that has the same long vowel sound. Underline the letter or letters that make the long vowel sound in the words you write.

pave	kind	bleach	loan	continue

6. note _____   9. tile _____

7. frame _____   10. blue _____

8. meek _____

Name _____

A. Read the draft model. Use the questions that follow the draft to help you think about ways to use strong, vivid words to create a clearer picture of what is happening.

Draft Model

   In the orchard, Hester and John met the scary soldiers. John wanted to leave, but Hester gave each soldier a nice apple.

---

1. What time of day is it? Would the orchard be scarier if the story took place at night?

2. Why are the soldiers there? What words can you use to describe what makes them scary?

3. What strong, vivid words can you use to describe how John and Hester feel about the soldiers?

4. Is there something about the soldiers that makes Hester want to give them apples? What words can you use to make this clearer?

B. Now revise the draft by adding precise, descriptive words and phrases that will help the reader visualize what is happening in the orchard.

_____

_____

_____

_____

_____

_____

_____

_____

Name _____

The student who wrote the paragraphs below used text evidence from two different sources to answer the question: *Which alliance do you think was better for the characters, Homer and Harold's alliance or Jonas and Sean's alliance? Use text evidence from two sources to support your argument.*

Even though Homer and Harold were fighting for their lives on a battlefield, Jonas and Sean's alliance was better for the characters than Homer and Harold's alliance. For one, Harold apparently didn't have much of an alliance with his brother. Harold could have avoided the war, but he wanted to leave. He did not want to take care of Homer anymore. And Homer did not actually save Harold. Homer did chase after him onto a battlefield, but Harold would have survived without Homer. Colonel Chamberlain offered the prisoners freedom if they fought, and Harold jumped at the chance. He would have survived.

School can be a battlefield, too, and sometimes it feels as if you are fighting for your life. If Jonas hadn't met Sean, he would probably not have found the courage to stand up to Ernesto. Sean probably wouldn't have, either. But their alliance gave them strength. Together, they wouldn't have to walk in fear of their enemies. They could walk through the trenches of school as a united force.

Reread the passage. Follow the directions below.

1. What is the writer's opinion? **Circle** the statement that introduces the claim.

2. How does the writer support his opinion? **Underline** supporting details that support the claim.

3. **Draw a box** around an example of strong word choice.

4. **Write** the subject and predicate of this sentence: For one, Harold apparently didn't have much of an alliance with his brother.

_____

Name _____

| classification | compartment | engulfs | flanked |
| maneuvering | obscure | species | submerged |

Finish each sentence using the vocabulary word provided.

1. **(classification)** The science teacher _____
_____ .

2. **(compartment)** The diving gear _____
_____ .

3. **(engulfs)** We can watch as the water _____
_____ .

4. **(flanked)** The security guards _____
_____ .

5. **(maneuvering)** It was going to take some careful _____
_____ .

6. **(obscure)** As the storm came closer, _____
_____ .

7. **(species)** The explorers wondered if the strange insect _____
_____ .

8. **(submerged)** The divers _____
_____ .

Name _____

Read the selection. Complete the main idea and key details graphic organizer.

Main Idea

Detail

Detail

Detail

Name _____

Read the passage. Use the reread strategy to help you understand new facts or difficult information.

Amazing Plant Discoveries

	Have you ever seen trees with exploding seedpods? Or rat-eating plants?
11	Do such things really exist? It seems as though we know a great deal about
26	our world. However, each year scientists discover many new kinds of
37	plants. These discoveries help us learn about how plants adapt to the
49	geography and environment in which they live.
56	**The Kew Gardens Discovery**
60	England's Kew Gardens is known for its gardens and its research. Their
72	botanists travel the world in search of new plant species. In 2009 they
85	made hundreds of great discoveries. Several were plants found in the rain
97	forests of West Africa. One discovery was a species of palm tree. It had
111	never been seen before. The botanists named it *Berlinia korupensis*. It was
123	named after the national park in which it was found.
133	*Berlinia korupensis* is an unusual tree. It is very tall. It reaches 140 feet
147	into the canopy of the rain forest. It also releases its seeds in a very violent
163	way.
164	Plants have different systems for releasing seeds. Some seeds are carried
175	by wind or float on water. Others may be transported on the backs of birds
190	or other animals. Some may drop to the ground in animal waste. Still
203	others require fire or a great deal of time to break down a hard outer shell.
219	The beautiful white flowers of this tree develop into foot-long seedpods.
230	Each pod contains two or three seeds. When the pods burst open, they
243	shoot the seeds into the air. The seeds travel like missiles.

Name

Rain forests are challenging places for plants to survive. Many trees and other plants compete for sunlight. They are all trying to reach the top of the canopy. The seeds of this tree travel far from the tree. That way they don't have to compete with the parent tree for sunlight. This gives the seeds the best chance of growing in this ecosystem.

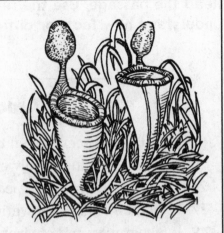

This is the rat-eating pitcher plant known as *Nepenthes attenboroughii.*

The Rat-Eating Pitcher Plant

In 2009 other botanists made another strange discovery. They were exploring a mountainous area in the Philippines. They had heard about an unusual pitcher plant from several missionaries. As the botanists approached a remote mountaintop, they saw the pitcher plants. They were one of the largest pitcher plant species in the world. These meat-eating plants were so large they could swallow a rat.

Carnivorous plants need to have a way to capture prey. They need to be able to digest it. They also must have a way to use what they have eaten. This plant has a sweet smell that attracts prey. It has a long tube that insects and small animals tumble into. It is so large it can hold a rat or mouse. Inside, sticky ribs keep the animal from escaping. Then, chemicals at the bottom digest it.

All plants need nitrogen to live. In most cases, the roots of plants absorb it from the soil. However, these pitcher plants grow where the soil is sandy and rocky. The soil contains little nitrogen. In order to survive, these plants must get nitrogen elsewhere. They get it from the insects and animals they "eat"!

Today, some people call this plant a rat-eating plant. Some say it is one of the ten most dangerous plants on the planet.

Regardless, the head of Kew Gardens says, "[T]here is so much of the plant world yet to be discovered." He might add, "and so much left for us to learn."

Name _____

A. Reread the passage and answer the questions.

1. How are the details in the first paragraph under the head "The Rat-Eating Pitcher Plant" connected?

_____

_____

2. How are the details in the second paragraph under the head "The Rat-Eating Pitcher Plant" connected?

_____

_____

3. How are the details in the third paragraph under the head "The Rat-Eating Pitcher Plant" connected?

_____

_____

4. What is the main idea of these first three paragraphs?

_____

_____

B. Work with a partner. Read the passage aloud. Pay attention to accuracy. Stop after one minute. Fill out the chart.

	Words Read	–	Number of Errors	=	Words Correct Score
First Read		–		=	
Second Read		–		=	

Name _____

Aquatic Plant Life

Aquatic plants, or plants that live under water, are called hydrophytes. Because they are partly or totally submerged, hydrophytes have adaptations for living in water. Their stems and leaves lack strength, allowing the plants to move freely in water. A hydrophyte's roots function mainly as an anchor rather than as a means of supplying nutrients. Finally, the leaves of each hydrophyte usually have a variety of shapes, allowing maximum absorption and photosynthesis.

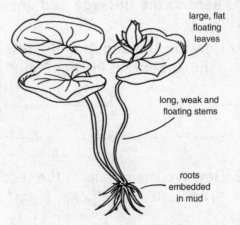

large, flat floating leaves

long, weak and floating stems

roots embedded in mud

A water lily is a hydrophyte. Its leaves, stem, and roots are adaptations for living in water.

Answer the questions about the text.

1. What features of expository text does this passage contain?

_____

_____

2. What does the heading tell you about the topic?

_____

3. What is the main idea of the text?

_____

_____

4. How does the diagram reinforce the concepts in the text?

_____

_____

Name _____

Answer the following questions about words with Greek roots.

1. The word *geography* contains two Greek roots. The root *geo* means "earth" and *graph* means "to draw, write, or make a picture." What do you think *geography* means in the following sentence?

   These discoveries help us learn about how plants adapt to the **geography** and environment in which they live.

   _____

   _____

2. *System* is a word with Greek origins that means "an organized whole." *Eco-* is a prefix that means "environment." What do you think *ecosystem* means in the following sentence?

   This gives the seeds the best chance of growing in this **ecosystem**.

   _____

   _____

3. If *botany* is the study of plants, what is a **botanist**?

   _____

   _____

4. If *canopy* comes from a Greek word that means "a curtain or covering over a bed," what do you think a **canopy** in a forest is?

   _____

   _____

Name _____

affect	bought	excuse
caught	except	there

A. Read each word below. Then choose a word from the box that has a similar spelling pattern and write it on the line.

1. misuse _____

2. affection _____

3. where _____

4. taught _____

5. adept _____

6. fought _____

B. Read each sentence. Write the underlined word on the line and circle the letters that spell the vowel sound in each syllable.

7. The study group had a good <u>effect</u> on his grade. _____

8. They wore <u>their</u> away uniforms to the game. _____

9. It was an <u>especially</u> steep hill to climb. _____

10. We expect that it will <u>probably</u> rain this weekend. _____

11. Singing on stage would <u>embarrass</u> the young girl. _____

12. His older brother would <u>accuse</u> him of borrowing too much. _____

Name _____

A. Read the draft model. Use the questions that follow the draft to help you think about ways to focus on the topic and add precise details.

Draft Model

There are many unusual rainforest plants. They are very different from the plants you would find in your backyard!

---

1. Which rainforest plant do you want to focus on?

2. What is different about this plant?

3. What details will help the reader visualize the plant and understand why it is unusual?

B. Now revise the draft by focusing on one type of rainforest plant. Provide rich, focused details about that plant and why it is unusual.

_____

_____

_____

_____

_____

_____

_____

_____

_____

_____

_____

Name _____

The student who wrote the paragraphs below used text evidence from two different sources to answer the question: *How are deep-sea explorers able to overcome the challenges of this extreme environment?*

Despite the extreme conditions of the deep sea—constant darkness, powerful water pressure, and extremely cold temperature—deep-sea explorers are able to investigate the darkest depths of the ocean by working together and using specialized equipment. Scientists from around the world work together to explore Earth's oceans, which are all really connected. For example, in 2002, thousands of scientists began the Census of Marine Life to list the oceans' plants and animals. Because the oceans are so vast, the scientists split into teams. Many scientists explored the shallow parts of the oceans, but others explored the deepest parts.

Scientists also use specialized equipment that can hold up to the extreme conditions of the deep sea. They take vehicles called submersibles down to the ocean floor. These submersibles have a big, clear viewing area, mechanical arms, lights, and cameras. The mechanical arms help scientists collect samples from the ocean, and the bright lights reveal the scenery. Scientists wouldn't be able to see out of the viewing area if there were no lights! Cameras and video recorders are used to take pictures of deep-sea habitats, which are home to many strange creatures.

Reread the passage. Follow the directions below.

1. **Circle** the statement that introduces the topic.

2. **Underline** supporting details that support the topic.

3. **Draw a box** around transitions used to show the relationship among ideas.

4. **Write** a compound sentence that on the line.

_____

_____

Name _____

cascaded	documentation	dynamic	plummeting
pulverize	scalding	shards	exerts

Write a complete sentence to answer each question below. In your answer, use the vocabulary word shown in bold.

1. What is an example of a **scalding** liquid?

   _____

2. Why should you be careful around **shards** of glass?

   _____

3. If you see an object **plummeting** from the sky, what is the object doing?

   _____

4. What happens to something if you **pulverize** it?

   _____

5. What kind of **documentation** shows your identity, or who you are?

   _____

6. When could you say a person **exerts** a large amount of energy?

   _____

7. What is a natural occurrence that could be described as **dynamic**?

   _____

8. Where in nature can you find water that has **cascaded**?

   _____

Name _____

**Read the selection. Complete the main idea and key details
graphic organizer.**

Main Idea
Detail
Detail
Detail

Name_____

Read the passage. Use the reread strategy to identify the main idea and key details.

Mount St. Helens

The Sleeping Giant

3	Mount St. Helens is a volcano. It had been thought of as one of the most
19	beautiful volcanic mountains in Washington State. Like a sleeping giant,
29	Mount St. Helens lay still for more than 100 years. On May 18, 1980, the
44	giant woke up with a boom. A strong earthquake shook beneath it.
56	At 8:32 A.M. that day, volcanologist David Johnston called his
66	colleagues at the U.S. Geological Survey (USGS). The USGS had set up a
79	base in Vancouver, Washington, to watch volcanic activity in the mountain
90	range. Johnston was watching Mount St. Helens from a camp on the
102	mountain. He said, "Vancouver, Vancouver, this is it!" Mount St. Helens
113	exploded. It caused one of the largest landslides ever recorded. The north
125	face of the mountain fell in the blast. Spirit Lake was buried in hundreds
139	of feet of debris. Trees were blown down like matchsticks. Johnston and
151	fifty-six people died in the blast. When the ash was still and the smoke
165	cleared, more than 240 miles of forest had been destroyed.

Warning Signs

177	There had been warning signs. In 1978 scientists at the USGS thought
189	that Mount St. Helens might blast again. It had a history of eruptions. On
203	March 20, 1980, an earthquake was recorded beneath Mount St. Helens.
214	Another quake was recorded three days later. After that, the quakes hit like
227	waves. There were about 15 per hour. By March 25, pilots flying over the
241	volcano saw cracks in the glaciers and a number of avalanches. The giant
254	could not sleep with the strong shakes of the earth below. Huge blasts of
268	steam in April and May led to the great blast on May 18.

Name _____

A Real-life Laboratory

Peter Frenzen flew over the blast zone after the eruption. Frenzen was an ecologist. An ecologist is a scientist who studies how plants and animals act with their environment. All he could see below was a scorched landscape and a "ghost forest" of ash. Still, Frenzen felt excited. He had studied how forests come back from natural disasters on another mountain. Now he had a new site to study forest recovery. Mount St. Helens became a real-life laboratory.

Frenzen walked around the blast zone and learned that much wildlife still lived. Small animals that live beneath the ground, such as mice and gophers, came out from the ash. Jerry Franklin was the scientist who led the research team at Mount St. Helens after the eruption. He also studied the survival

Mount St. Helens after its eruption in 1980

of species after a natural disturbance. He said that buried roots, bulbs, and seedlings were important in rebuilding forests. Because some plants had also survived on the mountain, they would create new habitats and start the recovery of the forests of Mount St. Helens. Large areas of the forest did come back to life as the summer progressed.

In 1982 Congress established a monument of 110,000 acres on Mount St. Helens. The monument protects the mountain from logging and allows the forest to regrow. Since then, trees and plants have spread across the landscape. They grow taller and denser each year. Writer and scientist Tim McNulty has called Mount St. Helens a lesson in hope. As long as nature is allowed to run, he says, it is a clock that keeps ticking.

Name _____

A. Reread the passage and answer the questions.

1. What are at least four key details in the third paragraph?

_____

_____

_____

_____

2. How are these details related to one another?

_____

_____

3. What is the main idea in the third paragraph?

_____

_____

B. Work with a partner. Read the passage aloud. Pay attention to phrasing and rate. Stop after one minute. Fill out the chart.

	Words Read	–	Number of Errors	=	Words Correct Score
First Read		–		=	
Second Read		–		=	

Name _____

Laki Volcano

Most people associate a volcanic eruption with scalding steam and hot lava. However, poisonous volcanic gases can cause Earth's temperatures to plunge. In the winter after Iceland's Laki volcano erupted in 1783, severely cold temperatures and volcanic gases spread throughout the northern hemisphere. Farm animals and crops in Iceland died from the poisonous gases and extreme temperatures. As a result, many people in Iceland died of starvation.

Robert Krimmel/Cascades Volcano Observatory/USGS

Volcanic gases from Laki blocked the sun and led to a very cold winter.

Answer the questions about the text.

1. How do you know this is narrative nonfiction?

_____

2. What is the text's main idea? List two details that support the main idea.

_____

_____

_____

_____

3. How would you improve the heading of the text?

_____

_____

4. What other features of narrative nonfiction are included in the passage?

_____

Name _____

Answer the questions about each of the following comparisons.

1. In the simile "Like a sleeping giant, Mount St. Helens lay still,"
   how is Mount St. Helens like a giant before the eruption?

   _____

   _____

2. In the simile "Trees were blown down like matchsticks," what force
   causes the trees to fall, and what does the simile tell you about it?

   _____

   _____

3. What does the simile "After that, the quakes hit like waves" say
   about the earthquakes?

   _____

   _____

4. What does the metaphor "the giant could not sleep with the strong
   shakes of the earth below" say about the volcano?

   _____

   _____

Name _____

A. Read the words below and listen for the *r*-controlled vowel sound. Put each word under the correct heading and underline the letters that stand for the *r*-controlled vowel sound.

torch	parched	search	sparkle
care	urge	wear	mourn

/är/ sound, as in *march*	/âr/ sound, as in *chair*	/ûr/ sound, as in *shirt*	/ôr/ sound, as in *fort*
_____	_____	_____	_____
_____	_____	_____	_____

B. Circle the correct word with an *r*-controlled vowel sound to complete each sentence. Then write the word on the line.

1. Don't spread that _____!

   mess   problem   rumor

2. I tried in _____ to study for the test.

   quiet   earnest   class

3. The judge spoke in _____.

   court   prose   private

4. My sister found a great _____ at the sale.

   deal   bargain   price

5. A class party was the _____ for perfect attendance.

   prize   event   reward

Name _____

A. Read the draft model. Use the questions that follow the draft to help you think about ways to give a distinct voice to the text.

Draft Model

I sometimes walk in the swamp near my home. In my high boots, I see frogs and trees in the fog. I usually walk alone. All I can hear is my steps in the water.

---

1. How can you change the first sentence to give it a particular "voice," or style and tone?

2. What does the narrator see and hear in the swamp? What could the narrator feel, taste, or smell in the swamp?

3. What words would help the reader understand how the narrator feels about being alone in the swamp? What vivid descriptions would show this?

B. Now revise the draft by adding words and phrases that help to develop the style and tone of the writing.

_____

_____

_____

_____

_____

_____

_____

_____

_____

_____

The student who wrote the paragraphs below used text evidence from two different sources to answer the question: *How does Donna O'Meara feel about the dangers of her job?*

One requirement of a volcano researcher's job is to be able to handle dangerous, life-threatening situations. Donna O'Meara not only handles this requirement; she loves it.

The dangers of being a volcano researcher are outweighed by Donna's love for art and science—and adventure. As an artist, she captures rare scenes that few people see. On her first trip to Kilauea volcano in Hawaii, she lowered herself onto a ledge to get a shot of orange lava pouring into the ocean. She knew she'd "boil in the lava/sea/steam cauldron below" if she fell, but she described the light as "magical," and she captured the "best lava show in town."

As a scientist, Donna feels that the information she gathers from her experiences will help develop understanding about volcanoes and save lives. Even after being stranded on a ledge on Mt. Stromboli in freezing temperatures amid flying, hot rocks, she believes she has "the best job on earth."

Reread the passage. Follow the directions below.

1. **Circle** the statement that introduces the topic.

2. **Underline** supporting details that support the topic.

3. **Draw a box** around the conclusion.

4. **Write** a complex sentence on the line.

_____

_____

_____

_____

Name _____

| basically | manufactured | salaries | fluctuate |
| formula | inventory | factors | available |

Use each pair of vocabulary words in a single sentence.

1. inventory, fluctuate

_____

_____

2. basically, salaries

_____

_____

3. formula, available

_____

_____

4. factors, manufactured

_____

_____

Name _____

**Read the selection. Complete the author's point of view
graphic organizer.**

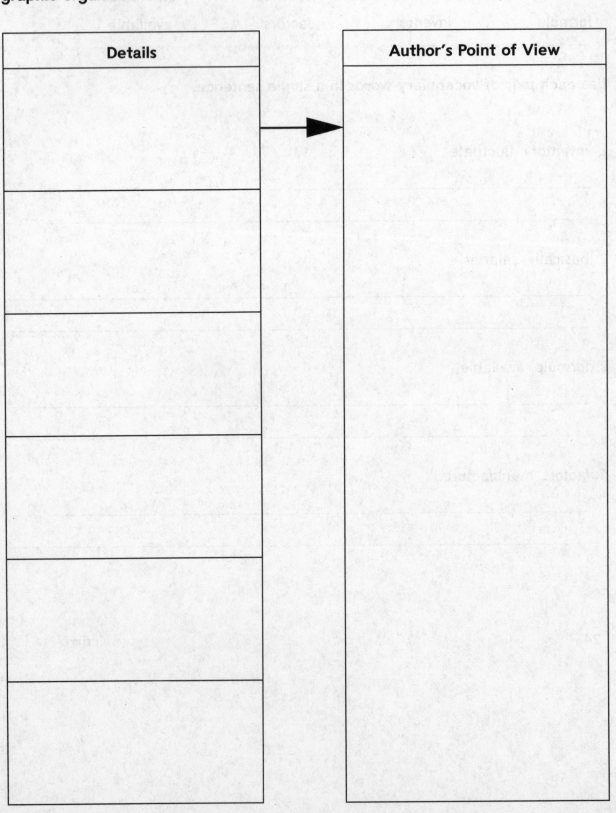

Details	Author's Point of View

Name_____

Read the passage. Use the reread strategy to help you understand difficult parts of the text.

The Ups and Downs of Inflation

10	From earning to spending and everything in between, inflation affects what happens to your money. As a result, inflation can have powerful
22	effects on the way you live.
28	Simply put, inflation is when prices rise. You are able to purchase fewer
41	items with each dollar you have. Inflation can affect everything you buy—
53	from a candy bar to a basketball to a car. Imagine that you receive the
68	same allowance two years in a row. If the price of video games doubles
82	from one year to the next, then you will have to save up twice as much to
99	buy a new game.

103	**Why, Oh Why?**
106	Economists study the way wealth is made, used, and shared among
117	people. Some economists say that inflation means there are "too many
128	dollars chasing too few goods." In this situation, there is a greater supply
141	of money than a supply of goods.
148	To understand this, picture an economy with only two goods, paper
159	money and skateboards. Imagine that one year a company cannot get
171	enough wheels for all the skateboards. With fewer skateboards to sell, each
183	one will be more valuable to buyers. They will be willing to pay more to
198	get one. This shortage of supply of goods can lead to what is called "cost-
213	push" inflation.
215	Another way prices can be pushed higher is if the government decides to
228	print lots more money. This also can cause inflation. If the money supply
241	is too large, the value of each dollar falls. When the value of the currency
256	decreases, prices rise.

Name _____

With inflation, the desire for goods and services is greater than the economy's ability to meet the demand. Sometimes the government spends more money than it gets from taxes. When governments pay their bills by printing more money instead of raising taxes, the effect is inflation. The new supply causes people to spend more money buying goods and services. If the demand is already high, more demand drives the prices higher.

People sometimes add to inflation as they try to protect themselves from it. If you have a job, you might ask for more pay. As a result, your employer might have to raise prices to pay for your higher wages. This leads to more inflation.

Spending Habits During Inflation

Inflation affects people differently depending on their income. Some people have incomes that stay the same. Some may have incomes that do not rise enough to match inflation. These people do not have the money to buy what they usually do. They may have to go without things. Sometimes inflation causes people to go into debt, or to borrow money to pay for their normal needs.

If people believe prices will keep rising, they may buy ahead of their need. If something you planned to get next year will cost more later, you may decide to get it right away. That thinking can lead people to spend more money than normal. During long periods of inflation, people tend to spend more of their income and save less. If you save today and inflation levels rise, your money will not be worth as much in the future. A dollar will still look like a dollar. It will still be called a dollar. However, during inflation it will take more dollars to pay for your wants and needs.

High inflation can be hard on people and nations. National leaders work to control extreme inflation, but stopping it can be a challenge. People often don't want the government to cut back on services or to raise taxes to pay for them. Something has to give.

In the United States, the Federal Open Market Committee (FOMC) tries to figure out ways to keep inflation low. This helps keep the U.S. economy strong.

Name _____

A. Reread the passage and answer the questions.

1. In the second paragraph, what does the author say happens during inflation?

_____

2. Are the main points that the author includes on the first page of the passage opinions or could they be proved by evidence? Are the author's words trying to convince readers to feel a certain way?

_____

_____

_____

3. In the text under the head "Spending Habits During Inflation," what are three ways the author says people change their spending during inflation?

_____

_____

_____

4. Based on the information in the text and the words and details the author uses, what is the author's point of view about inflation? Is this point of view biased or objective?

_____

_____

B. Work with a partner. Read the passage aloud. Pay attention to rate. Stop after one minute. Fill out the chart.

	Words Read	–	Number of Errors	=	Words Correct Score
First Read		–		=	
Second Read		–		=	

Name _____

Creating Your Own Budget

To begin creating a monthly budget, write down your planned income from work and other sources. Next, below that, write your planned expenses for essential needs (such as food). Then, write your planned expenses for other things you want (such as a new phone). At the end of the month, write your actual income and expenses. Figure out the differences between your plans and what you really earned and spent. Do you need to manage your money better? Do you need to spend more on needs and less on wants?

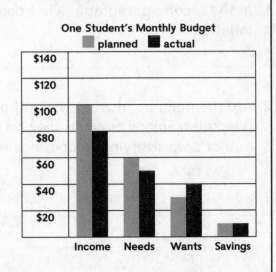

One Student's Monthly Budget

planned actual

$140
$120
$100
$80
$60
$40
$20

Income Needs Wants Savings

Answer the questions about the text.

1. How do you know this is expository text?

_____

_____

2. What text features does this text include?

_____

3. Is the heading a strong one for this text? Why or why not?

_____

_____

4. What information does the bar graph give you?

_____

_____

Name _____

Read each passage. Write a definition of the word in bold using context clues and the meaning of the root word.

1. From earning to spending and everything in between, **inflation** affects what happens to your money. Simply put, inflation is when prices rise. You are able to purchase fewer items with each dollar you have.

   root word: inflate

   _____

2. With fewer skateboards to sell, each one will be more **valuable** to buyers.

   root word: value

   _____

3. This **shortage** of supply can lead to what is called "cost-push" inflation.

   root word: short

   _____

4. Another way prices can be pushed higher is if the **government** decides to print lots more money.

   root word: govern

   _____

5. With inflation, the desire for goods and services is greater than the economy's **ability** to meet the demand.

   root word: able

   _____

A. Read each sentence. Circle the pair of words that should be joined together to become a closed compound. Then write the compound word on the line.

1. We drove north west to visit our cousins. _____

2. I got new glasses because the doctor told me I am near sighted. _____

3. How many sea shells did you collect at the beach? _____

4. In just a few months she will become a teen ager. _____

5. There was so much ice that I had to help scrape the wind shield. _____

B. Read each pair of words in the row and circle the pair that should be hyphenated. Then write the hyphenated compound on the line.

6. water melon   question mark   self respect   _____

7. finger nail   old fashioned   teen ager   _____

8. wading pool   full time   eye lid   _____

9. all star   science fiction   team mate   _____

10. twenty five   post office   farm yard   _____

Name _____

A. Read the draft model. Use the questions that follow the draft to help you think about how you can add transitions to connect related ideas.

Draft Model

Each year I go through my clothes and choose many to donate to charity. I rarely wear these items. Other people could use them.

---

1. How can you add a sentence using the transition *for instance* to show an example of the types of clothes that are donated?

2. How can you use a transition such as *also, in addition,* or *another* to add an idea that is similar to one already in the draft?

3. What transition can you use to explain why the speaker rarely wears the items? Make sure your transition connects a cause and an effect.

B. Now revise the draft by adding transitions that connect related ideas.

_____

_____

_____

_____

_____

_____

Name _____

The student who wrote the paragraphs below used text evidence from two different sources to answer the question: *Should the government play a large role in running the economy?*

> The government should play a role in running the economy. Currently, the Federal Reserve System has the power to adjust interest rates, and this power keeps the country's economy running like a well-oiled machine. If the government didn't control interest rates, the forces of supply and demand could become out of balance and stop the economy from running smoothly.
>
> The forces of supply and demand can sometimes be affected by things that are out of our control. For example, bad weather can destroy crops and reduce the number of certain fruits or vegetables that are available. Low availability causes higher prices. The federal government can stop prices from rising too fast or becoming too high.
>
> Interest rates apply when people borrow money. These rates are determined by supply and demand. When interest rates are too high, people are less likely to spend money, which can result in companies not making enough money to pay their employees. By lowering the interest rate, the government helps people make bigger purchases, which helps industries grow and provide jobs.

Reread the passage. Follow the directions below.

1. **Circle** the statement that introduces the student's claim.

2. **Underline** relevant details that support the claim.

3. **Draw a box** around transition words.

4. **Write** a sentence in which the writer avoids a comma splice.

_____

_____

_____

Name _____

artifact   communal   derived   inscription

millennium   stationery   utilize   yields

Finish each sentence using the vocabulary word provided.

1. **(inscription)** In order to know why the statue was built, we _____

   _____.

2. **(communal)** After we got our food, we _____

   _____.

3. **(derived)** Some information about the ancient civilization was _____

   _____.

4. **(artifact)** The explorers found _____

   _____.

5. **(yields)** The farmers were happy because _____

   _____.

6. **(stationery)** We need to write a letter, but _____

   _____.

7. **(utilize)** In order to build something, you need _____

   _____.

8. **(millennium)** After a thousand years, _____

   _____.

Name _____

Read the selection. Complete the problem and solution graphic organizer.

Problem	Solution

Name_____

Read the passage. Use the ask and answer questions strategy before, during, and after each section.

The Mysterious Olmecs

12	The Olmecs were an ancient people who lived around 1200–400 B.C. in Middle America. Today we call that area Mexico and Central America.
24	There is a lot that is mysterious about the Olmecs. We know that they
38	made their own written language and calendars. But their systems of
49	language and numbers were difficult, and all we can do is make a guess
63	about what they mean. The Olmecs are well known for their huge rock
76	sculptures. Yet we don't know what the sculptures stand for or why
88	they were made. One thing we do know is that the Olmecs were a very
103	complicated people. We see their mark on cultures that came later such as
116	the Mayans and Aztecs.
120	The name Olmec means "people of rubber country." They lived where
131	rubber trees grew. It seems that the Olmecs were the first people to make
145	what we think of as rubber. They mixed vine juice with a milk-like liquid
159	from the trees. With this mixture, they made balls that could bounce high.
172	They used the balls to play games. Later, other cultures continued to play
185	ball games and found more ways to use rubber. The Olmecs' discovery
197	may be why we use rubber today.

204	**Early Writing in the Americas**
209	Archaeologists have proof that the Olmecs were the first people in the
221	Americas to write. Yet the Olmecs' early writings are a mystery. No one
234	has been able to break their written code.
242	Scientists discovered an important stone in Mexico that dates back to
253	about 900 B.C. Writing is carved into the rock. More pictures and symbols
266	were found on statues and masks. One rock slab has 465 carvings. We
279	do know that Olmec writings included calendar symbols. Large standing
289	stones were carved or painted with important events.

Name _____

A Matter of Time

Olmec calendars combined two different calendars. Priests made the calendars to keep track of ceremonies. One calendar had 260 days. They made another calendar that had 360 days for other events. The two calendars together were called the Long Count calendar. Long Count dates contained five simple numbers made up of lines and dots. The dates also contained the number zero. The Olmecs represented zero with a shell-shaped drawing. Archaeologists credit the Olmecs with inventing zero.

The Amazing Zero

The Olmecs used a base-20 counting system. They wrote separate numbers from 1–20, just as we do for 1–10 today. In order to make their system work, they needed to invent a zero.

The idea of zero is common to us. However, most ancient people did not understand it. It is really a very complex idea. Sometimes zero serves as a placeholder to explain other numbers. Zero also stands on its own as a number. The Olmecs understood that.

Stone Sculptures

Huge stone faces were found at several Olmec sites. These strange stone carvings range in size from five to nine feet tall. The images all have grim, flat faces. Each head wears what seems to be a helmet. No one knows why.

The purpose of the stone heads is unknown. People think the carvings may be of Olmec culture had many classes of people. Leaders would have ruled over the artisans and laborers. Maybe they demanded the images be made.

We still have a lot to learn about the Olmecs. Their written language, calendars, rubber-making techniques, and art all point to an early, advanced culture. Researchers have many more mysteries to unravel as they study the Olmec people. Perhaps the Olmecs' greatest contributions are yet to come.

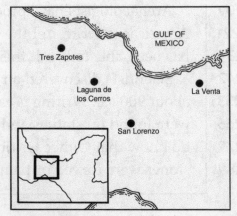

Olmec sites

Name _____

A. Reread the passage and answer the questions.

1. How did the Olmecs solve the problem of keeping track of their ceremonies as well as other events?

   _____

   _____

2. What problem did the Olmecs solve by inventing the zero?

   _____

   _____

3. What problem do researchers today have regarding the Olmecs? How might researchers solve this problem in the future?

   _____

   _____

   _____

   _____

B. Work with a partner. Read the passage aloud. Pay attention to rate and accuracy. Stop after one minute. Fill out the chart.

	Words Read	–	Number of Errors	=	Words Correct Score
First Read		–		=	
Second Read		–		=	

Name _____

The Moors' Influence on Western Europe

In 711, the Moors crossed into Spain. They remained there until 1492.
During their 780 years in Spain, the Moors influenced all of Western Europe,
not just Spain. They made agricultural and architectural advancements,
but their greatest influence was intellectual. They built more than seventy
libraries in the city of Cordoba alone. Muslims, Jews, and Christians
gathered in Moorish cities to study philosophy, science, and medicine. After
foreign invaders conquered Spain, some great Moorish libraries remained.

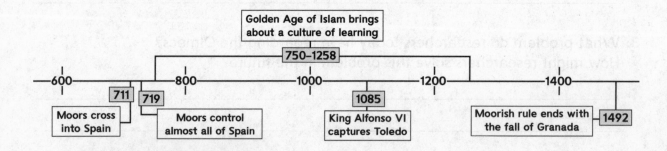

Answer the questions about the text.

1. What features of expository text does this passage contain?

   _____

   _____

2. What does the heading tell you about the topic?

   _____

3. How does the text expand on the idea in the heading?

   _____

   _____

4. Give one example of how the timeline supports a fact in the text.

   _____

   _____

Name _____

Use context clues and the information about Latin roots below each passage to decide what each word in bold means. Write the definition on the line.

1. "It is really a very **complex** idea."
   The Latin prefix *com-* means "together." The Latin root *plexus* means "braided or twisted." In the sentence above, what does *complex* mean?

   _____

2. "Sometimes zero **serves** as a placeholder to explain other numbers." The Latin root *serv* means "to perform the duties of." In the sentence above, what does *serves* mean?

   _____

3. "These strange stone carvings range in size from five to nine feet tall. The **images** all have grim, flat faces."
   The Latin root *imag* means "likeness." In the sentence above, what does *images* mean?

   _____

4. "Leaders would have ruled over the **artisans** and laborers."
   The Latin root *art* means "skill." In the sentence above, what does *artisans* mean?

   _____

5. "Leaders would have ruled over the artisans and **laborers**."
   The Latin root *lab* means "work." In the sentence above, what does *laborers* mean?

   _____

Name _____

A. Read each sentence. Fill in the blanks by writing the plural form of the word in parentheses.

1. (shelf) Several of the _____ were full of books.

2. (knife) How many forks and _____ do we need to set the table?

3. (echo) The _____ of thunder filled the air.

4. (thief) Police warned about _____ near the train station.

5. (life) This medical device can save many _____.

6. (wolf) The pack of _____ traveled together.

7. (potato) My cousin helped me peel all the _____.

B. To make an irregular noun ending in -*um* plural, change the -*um* to -*a*. Write the plural form for each noun.

8. medium _____

9. bacterium _____

10. datum _____

Name _____

A. Read the draft model. Use the questions that follow the draft to help you think about ways to provide supporting details that will tell the reader more about the main idea.

Draft Model

Inventors built the first computer to do calculations. Now people also use computers for research and to keep in touch. These machines have Internet and word processing software.

---

1. When were computers first invented?

2. How big were the first computers? What kinds of calculations did they perform?

3. What details could be added to explain how and why computers changed?

4. How is society affected by the wide availability of the Internet and of word processing software?

B. Now revise the draft by adding details that will help the reader learn more about how computers have changed over time.

_____

_____

_____

_____

_____

_____

_____

Name _____

The student who wrote the paragraphs below used text evidence from two different sources to answer the question: *How does the* Epic of Gilgamesh *differ from examples of Mesopotamian writing discussed in* The Technology of Mesopotamia?

The Epic of Gilgamesh is very different from the examples of Mesopotamian writing discussed in *The Technology of Mesopotamia.* That selection tells that the people of Mesopotamia first used cuneiform to record information about agriculture and the economy. They had symbols for objects and numbers, but they didn't have enough symbols to tell stories or record the spoken word. As cuneiform got more complex, Mesopotamians came up with symbols for different sounds. Then they could use cuneiform to record the languages the Mesopotamian people spoke.

The Epic of Gilgamesh was discovered in the remains of an ancient Assyrian library. Researchers pieced together fragments of brittle, dusty stone and translated the cuneiform. *The Epic of Gilgamesh* was different from any other stone tablets they found in the library. It told of a great hero and his exciting adventures. It could have only been written down after cuneiform was advanced enough to reproduce the spoken word. Thanks to cuneiform, people can still read the *Epic of Gilgamesh,* thousands of years after it was written down.

Reread the passage. Follow the directions below.

1. **Underline** the text evidence that tells what cuneiform was used for at first.

2. **Draw a circle** around the words that give you sensory details about what it must have been like working with the fragments of the stone tablets.

3. **Draw a box** around the part of the conclusion that refers back to the topic.

4. **Write** a proper noun and a common noun from the selection.

_____

_____

Name _____

| aspiring | foundation | restrict | withstood |
| speculation | principal | promote | preceded |

Use each pair of vocabulary words in a single sentence.

1. aspiring, foundation

_____

_____

2. speculation, restrict

_____

_____

3. principal, promote

_____

_____

4. withstood, preceded

_____

_____

Name _____

Read the selection. Complete the compare and contrast graphic organizer.

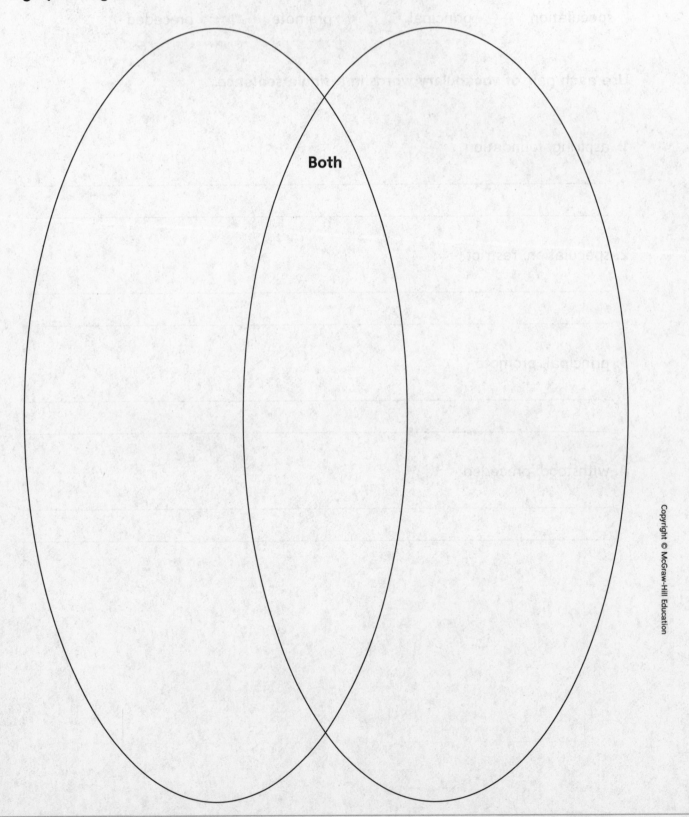

Both

Name _____

**Read the passage. Use the ask and answer questions
strategy before, during, and after each section.**

What is a Democracy?

The United States of America is a democracy. Most people have thought
so since the nation began. But what does democracy mean? The Greek
prefix *demo-* means "people." The Greek root word *cracy* means "rule."
So, the word *democracy* suggests a government ruled by the people.
What exactly does this mean in a country like ours?

The Pursuit of Liberty

When the Puritans made their way to America, they wanted to have the
liberty to make their own choices. They left England to seek freedom of
religion. In America, they had a new problem. They had to build a new
government, but they still wanted to protect their freedom. They came
up with the idea of gathering together the people in a town to make key
decisions. These gatherings were known as town meetings. Laws were
made with the people's interests in mind.

Town-Hall Meetings

In Puritan times, town halls were built in order to take care of town
business. Sometimes, town halls were used for worship services as
well, since they were the largest buildings in town. Early settlers looked
forward to town meeting days. The meetings were more than a time to
vote. Without telephones or other ways to keep people in touch, the town
meetings were also social gatherings for the public.

As New England grew, people with common interests settled in small
towns together, just as the Puritans did. That meant that for the most
part, everyone living in a town had the same goals. Voters met to solve
problems for the good of all, making it possible for people to participate
directly in legislation. In small towns this form of democracy worked.

Line counts (left margin): 12, 24, 35, 46, 56, 60, 73, 86, 100, 111, 126, 136, 143, 145, 159, 169, 181, 194, 207, 215, 226, 239, 253, 266

Name _____

In many small communities today, the town meeting is still important. Not only is it still a good way of governing, but it is a tradition that many people see as a symbol of democracy.

Two Kinds of Democracy

The kind of democracy that takes place in town-hall meetings is known as "direct democracy." In early New England, direct democracy worked very well. Members of a community made important decisions together. Everyone had a say in the process. However, as small towns grew larger, it became harder for everyone to meet in one place and take part in legislation. As the need for government extended to cities, states, and the nation as a whole, the town meeting became less practical.

Fortunately, direct democracy is not the only form of democracy. Another form is known as "representative democracy." This means that people vote for leaders who make laws for them. These representatives govern in place of the people. This form of democracy is necessary when there are too many people and too many different interests for everyone to participate directly.

Democracy in the United States Today

What system of democracy does the United States have today? Our nation is much too large for all to participate directly in decision-making. So, our national government must use the representative form of democracy. State governments use representative government as well. If they are small enough, some local governments do still govern with direct democracy, just as they did in early America. However, in the country as a whole, this is the exception today.

Some people might say that a representative democracy is not as pure a form as a direct democracy. However, both forms try to preserve freedom for all and equality in decision-making.

Direct Democracy	Representative Democracy
1. Works best in towns with small populations.	1. Works for towns, cities, and the nation with large populations.
2. Allows each voter to speak his/her mind.	2. Citizens elect people to represent their ideas about laws and government.
3. Allows voters to make decisions directly for themselves.	3. Representatives discuss the issues and make decisions for the people they represent.
4. Value is placed on personal freedom and political equality.	4. Value is placed on personal freedom and political equality.

Name _____

A. Reread the passage and answer the questions.

1. How are direct democracy and representative democracy similar?

_____

_____

2. What is the most significant difference between direct democracy and representative democracy?

_____

_____

_____

3. Why can some local governments still use direct democracy today, while state and national governments use representative democracy?

_____

_____

_____

_____

B. Work with a partner. Read the passage aloud. Pay attention to rate and accuracy. Stop after one minute. Fill out the chart.

	Words Read	–	Number of Errors	=	Words Correct Score
First Read		–		=	
Second Read		–		=	

Name _____

The U.S. Supreme Court

The Supreme Court is the highest court in our nation. The Court hears cases that are brought before it and interprets the Constitution. The Supreme Court can decide that a law passed by Congress is unconstitutional or constitutional. It can also tell a state that one of its laws violates the Constitution. Supreme Court members are chosen by the president and confirmed by Congress. They serve until they choose to retire. The Supreme Court is comprised of eight associate justices and one chief justice.

U.S. Supreme Court Justices in 2011	
Name	**Began serving**
Antonin Scalia	1986
Anthony M. Kennedy	1988
Clarence Thomas	1991
Ruth Bader Ginsburg	1993
Stephen G. Breyer	1994
John G. Roberts (Chief Justice)	2005
Samuel A. Alito, Jr.	2006
Sonia Sotomayor	2009
Elena Kagan	2010

Answer the questions about the text.

1. What features of expository text does this passage contain?

_____

_____

2. What is the topic of the text? How do you know?

_____

3. The chart gives evidence of what fact that is not stated in the text?

_____

_____

Name _____

Read each sentence below from "What is a Democracy?" and the meaning of each prefix. Write the meaning of the word in bold on the first line. Then use that word in a sentence of your own.

1. "The **United** States of America is a democracy."
   The Latin prefix *uni-* means "as one."

   Meaning: _____

   Sentence: _____

2. "Without **telephones** or other ways to keep people in touch, the town meetings were also social gatherings for the public."
   The Greek prefix *tele-* means "distant, far apart."

   Meaning: _____

   Sentence: _____

3. "Voters met to solve problems for the good of all, making it possible for people to participate directly in **legislation**."
   The Latin prefix *leg-* means "law."

   Meaning: _____

   Sentence: _____

4. "As the need for government **extended** to cities, states, and the nation as a whole, the town meeting became less practical."
   In *extended*, the Latin prefix *ex-* means "out."

   Meaning: _____

   Sentence: _____

Name _____

A. Write the correct -ed and -ing form of each verb.

Verb	+ ed	+ ing
1. orbit	_____	_____
2. patrol	_____	_____
3. confide	_____	_____
4. regret	_____	_____
5. accuse	_____	_____

**B. Read each sentence and circle the word that correctly uses
the inflectional ending. Then write the word on the line.**

6. We watched the cats as they _____ for mice in the yard.

    a. huntted   **b.** hunted   **c.** hunnted

7. The mirror was _____ the silver frame.

    a. surrounding   **b.** surroundding   **c.** surroundinng

8. The heat in the closed room was _____.

    a. stifleing   **b.** stiffling   **c.** stifling

9. Travelers _____ to the old map to find their way to the cave.

    a. reffered   **b.** refered   **c.** referred

10. Cold water _____ us after the long, difficult hike.

    a. revivved   **b.** revived   **c.** reviveed

Name _____

A. Read the draft model. Use the questions that follow the draft to help you think about what supporting details can be added to tell the reader more about the topic.

Draft Model

Last week, our class voted. Kids were on the ballot. Carla promised many things. I voted for her. She won!

---

1. What office was the class voting for?

2. Who exactly was on the ballot?

3. What exactly did Carla promise?

4. Why did the narrator choose to vote for Carla?

B. Now revise the draft by adding details to provide important information about the class election.

_____

_____

_____

_____

_____

_____

_____

Name _____

The student who wrote the paragraphs below used text evidence from two different sources to answer the question: *Should children who are not old enough to vote be allowed to propose new laws?*

> Children who are not old enough to vote should be allowed to propose *ideas* for new laws to their local representative. In 1787, our three-branch system of government was established in the U.S. Constitution. It states that the legislative branch passes laws, approves treaties, and creates spending bills. So these representatives are the people who can officially propose a law, but an *idea* for a law can, and should, be able to come from anyone, young or old.
>
> Adults aren't the only ones who have good ideas. Children come up with ideas for helpful laws, too. For example, after he fell off his bike, young Steve Kresky came up with the idea for a law that requires bicycle riders to wear helmets. He and his father contacted Maria Ortiz, a member of his state assembly. Along with representatives in the state senate, assembly members can make state laws. Ms. Ortiz agreed with Steve and his father, and she proposed a plan for a new law.
>
> So anyone—young or old—who has a good idea for a new law should contact the local state representative.

Reread the passage. Follow the directions below.

1. Should children be able to propose a law? **Circle** the statement that introduces the claim.

2. How does the writer support and develop the claim? **Underline** relevant details that support the claim.

3. **Draw a box** around the sentence that summarizes the claim.

4. **Write** a singular and plural noun on the line.

_____

Name _____

alcove	commerce	domestic	exotic
fluent	stifling	upheaval	utmost

Write a complete sentence to answer each question below. In your answer, use the vocabulary word in bold.

1. Why might a car not be parked in an **alcove**? _____

   _____

2. Where would you likely find **commerce** taking place? _____

   _____

3. What **domestic** item do you use that ancient people probably used? _____

   _____

4. Why is a dog not considered an **exotic** pet? _____

   _____

5. Why is it helpful to be **fluent** in Italian if you are visiting Italy? _____

   _____

6. What can make you feel better on a day when the heat is **stifling**? _____

   _____

7. When might an **upheaval** occur? _____

   _____

8. What is of **utmost** importance if you have a test coming up? _____

   _____

Name _____

Read the selection. Complete the details and point of view graphic organizer.

Details		Point of View
	→	

Name _____

Read the passage. Use the make predictions strategy to make logical guesses about what will happen next.

Kush, A Land of Archers

	The morning air had turned hot and steamy. Swatting the insects
11	feasting on my arms, I sat with ears tuned to the hills not far from the
27	Nile River. The clamor of battle still echoed in my head. Fighting was
40	not uncommon in the land of Kush. Egypt's jealous pharaohs to the north
53	often tried to rule my land.
59	Some people called our land Nubia, the land of gold. Foreigners
70	considered our gold a prize. Neighboring kingdoms often tried to rule us
82	in order to own our gold, iron, and precious stones.
92	However, our army of archers was widely known for strength and skill.
104	Bows and arrows were our weapons of war. The Kush army had been
117	victorious against the most recent invasion. Sadly, we did not always
128	triumph. The Kush gold mines were always at stake.
137	Running my fingers through the dirt, I began sketching the battle I
149	had heard from weeks past. I was forbidden to observe, even from the
162	sidelines. At twelve, the leaders declared I was too young to see for
175	myself. However, my memories of the distant drums punctuating the
185	sounds of the battle strongly fueled my curiosity. I quickly outlined
196	muscular archers launching their arrows into enemy lines. I imagined
206	myself in the field of archers. If only I could be there with my father
221	and brothers.
223	Father assigned me the farm chores and protection of the household
234	during any invasions. Even with those responsibilities, I made time for
245	target practice every day. My eldest brother had given me his old bow and
259	generously taught me the basics of archery. He said I was a natural archer.

Name _____

We looked forward to the annual "Festival of Many Villages." People gathered from all around, bringing delicious food. Potters brought their work to trade or sell. Musicians played and people danced. We enjoyed feasting and celebrating for several days.

The most important part to me was the great competition. Archers of all ages came to demonstrate their skill. The best athletes earned recognition. This season, I waited anxiously for the festival. I was nervous because I planned to enter the contest for the first time.

When the festival arrived, families flocked to the place where whole villages of people gathered. You could spot the women's brightly colored dresses from a distance.

"Mother, today you will be proud of me," I said as we walked toward the crowd. "I plan to compete in the archery contest." At first Mother looked surprised. I had not told her of my plan. She smiled at me with understanding.

"Oh, little Markos, give yourself time to grow!" my older brother wheedled, ruffling my hair with his oversized hands.

Ignoring him, I walked with purpose to the archery field. Drummers began pounding their rhythms while people gathered. The village leader announced the contestants' names, one by one.

Finally, I heard my name. I advanced to the center of the field with trembling hands, fighting back my fear. As the drums beat, I lifted my bow, or *kiniosha*, and drew the arrow back with care. The drum rhythms grew more rapid, while villagers chanted and stomped.

I took aim, aware that I could no longer delay. "Zing!" I felt the release. My eyes followed the arrow into the vivid blue sky and downward to the ground. When I ran toward the target, the villagers began chanting my name. My arrow had plunged into the most distant target of all. Only the experts' arrows had landed there!

Now I knew my future in the army would come true. Someday I would protect the land, treasure, and people of Kush. "Markos the Archer" sounded just right.

Name _____

A. Reread the passage and answer the questions.

1. Who is narrating the story?

   _____

2. How do you know which point of view (first-person or third-person) is used in the story?

   _____

   _____

   _____

3. What do you learn about the archery competition because of who the narrator is?

   _____

   _____

   _____

   _____

B. Work with a partner. Read the passage aloud. Pay attention to expression. Stop after one minute. Fill out the chart.

	Words Read	–	Number of Errors	=	Words Correct Score
First Read		–		=	
Second Read		–		=	

Name _____

Hasina, Fabric Maker of Deir el-Medina

"Hasina, please improve the stitching of this fabric," my boss Amisi tells me gently. "This cloth will eventually become a robe for the Pharaoh's son." My name, Hasina, means "good" in Egyptian, and I am proud of my name. I try to be good at my work as a fabric maker in my city of Deir el-Medina. "Of course. It must be perfect for our future king," I say. In my country, many women, like me, work outside of the home. Tomorrow, however, I will clean my house, cook, and keep my family "nefer," or pure and beautiful—my most important job.

Answer the questions about the text.

1. What details in the text place the plot in a historical setting?

   _____

   _____

   _____

2. How does Hasina's use of foreign words make her seem like a
   real character from history?

   _____

   _____

   _____

3. What does the text tell you about women of the time?

   _____

   _____

   _____

Name _____

A. Read each of the following excerpts from the passage. Then explain how the tone of the sentence would change if the word in bold were replaced by the word in parentheses.

1. Archers of all ages came to demonstrate their skill. The best athletes earned **recognition** (glory).

   _____

   _____

2. At first Mother looked **surprised** (amazed).

   _____

   _____

3. "Oh, little Markos, give yourself time to grow!" my older brother **wheedled** (pleaded), ruffling my hair with his oversized hands.

   _____

   _____

4. Ignoring him, I walked with **purpose** (boldness) to the archery field.

   _____

   _____

B. Write a few sentences explaining whether the word in bold has a positive or negative connotation and why.

5. "**Foreigners** considered our gold a prize."

   _____

   _____

   _____

Name _____

**Read each sentence. Circle the two-syllable words that have
a closed syllable.**

1. My mom loves to bake pumpkin seeds.

2. Our car's muffler needs some maintenance.

3. For the election, we wrote each ballot by hand.

4. Our pantry is full of great food for the holiday.

5. The prince inherited a large kingdom.

6. I chose a ribbon necklace to match my dress.

7. The dad took a snapshot of his son playing catch.

8. She took time to ponder why the land was barren.

9. The garment was created with an expensive fabric.

10. The brick dwelling was built extremely fast.

Name _____

A. Read the draft model. Use the questions that follow the draft to help you think about ways to make the conclusion stronger.

Draft Model

It was time for Mario to return home. As he boarded the airplane, he turned and waved back to us. He was now truly part of our family.

---

1. How might the conclusion help to clarify previous events in the story?

2. What descriptive words and phrases can you add to show the intensity of Mario's and the family's feelings?

3. What details would help make the conclusion more interesting or surprising?

B. Now revise the draft by adding details that will help create an interesting, satisfying conclusion to the story.

_____

_____

_____

_____

_____

_____

_____

Name _____

The student who wrote the paragraphs below used text evidence from two different sources to respond to the prompt: *Based on what you read about Roman aqueducts, write a short narrative about an ancient Roman showing a newcomer around the city and explaining the aqueducts to him or her.*

My friend gazed at the beautiful fountain. It was only her second day in Rome, and everything seemed new to her.

"Where does this water come from?" she asked. It's so clear. Is this Tiber River water?"

I smiled. I like bragging about my city. "Did you notice the pipe carrying water into the stone basin in my kitchen this morning?" I asked proudly.

"Yes. Where does the water come from?"

"That water flows from a mountain lake more than one hundred miles away," I answered. "Aqueducts carry that water to us. They start in the mountains and stretch all the way into the city. The water moves downhill at precise angles to keep the flow of water stable on its long journey."

"How lucky you are to have all of that water brought in fresh from such a long way away!"

"Not just me," I beamed. "I'm just a citizen of Rome. Everyone in my neighborhood shares that same water source."

"That's what I mean!" she laughed. "How lucky you are to be a citizen of this amazing city!"

Reread the passage. Follow the directions below.

1. **Draw a box** around a sentence that helps develop a character.

2. **Underline** an example of dialogue.

3. **Circle** the text evidence that describes the guest's reaction to the narrator's explanation of Rome's aqueducts.

4. **Write** a plural noun and a collective noun.

_____

Name _____

benefit	deftly	derision	eaves
expertise	impudence	legacy	symmetry

Use each pair of vocabulary words in a single sentence.

1. benefit, expertise

_____

_____

2. deftly, symmetry

_____

_____

3. impudence, derision

_____

_____

4. legacy, eaves

_____

_____

Name _____

Read the selection. Complete the details and point of view graphic organizer.

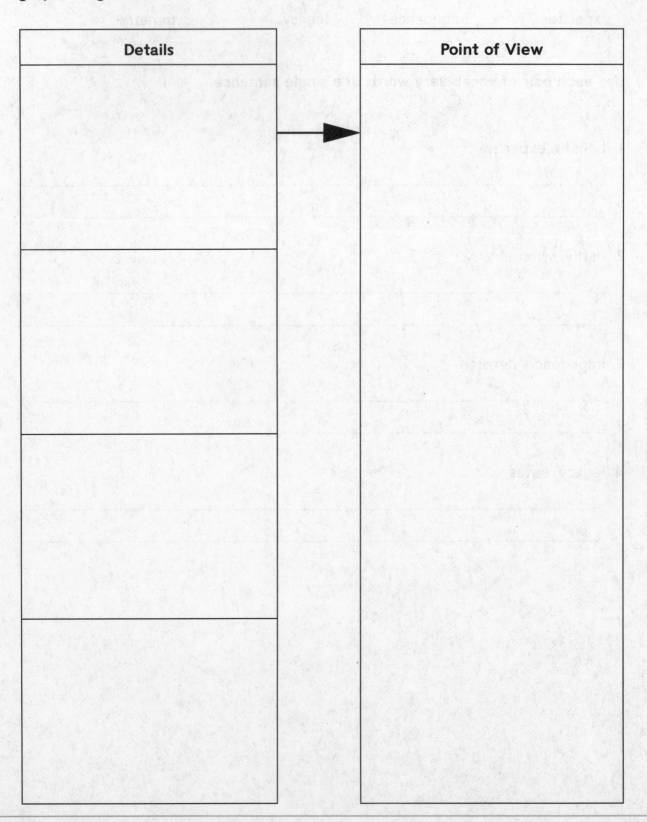

Details	Point of View

Name _____

Read the passage. Use the make predictions strategy to make logical guesses about what will happen next.

Approaching Zero

	Basu counted the steps, doing quick measurements as he walked along
11	the south bank of India's Ganges River, kicking up the hot, dusty ground.
24	He had arisen before daybreak, and the sun was now rising in the east.
38	By his calculations, he had walked 12,563 steps and covered about
49	one-quarter of the distance from his small village. By the time the sun was
63	directly overhead, he should finally reach the university at Patna. There he
75	hoped to find Aryabhata. Perhaps the great mathematician could help him
86	with the questions he'd been pondering: How do you measure the passing
98	of time and days? How do you determine the circumference of Earth? How
111	far away is the moon?
116	From what Basu had heard, Aryabhata had all of the answers, but the
129	master did not like to be disturbed. Basu's parents had warned him not to
143	go. "Why would a wise scholar want to waste his time with a twelve-year-
157	old boy?" his father had chided. Basu had a burning desire to study math
170	and to one day write a book like *Aryabhatiya*, Aryabhata's masterpiece.
181	According to the local scholars, the book described the earth as a
193	sphere that rotated around the sun, and it explained mathematics, time,
204	astronomy, and other mysteries of the universe.
211	Basu dragged a stick along the dirt, drawing a line. Was it a straight line
226	between where he just was and where he was going? He posed question
239	after question to himself to pass the time, keeping a running step count as
253	he went—18,231. The sun was just where Basu expected, casting a long
266	shadow from his stick.

Finally, just as the sun was overhead, Basu spotted a man crouched on a mat by a small, low table. He could see the man was furiously writing with a long iron spike that he dipped in ink, inscribing on the surface of hardened palm leaves. Basu held his breath and took quiet, short steps, cutting the remaining distance in half, and then in half again. Finally, he was standing beside Aryabhata. Basu was so close, he could see the mysterious numbers and symbols.

Basu was invisible to Aryabhata, who was immersed in his thoughts, but just then a beetle flew off the spike and landed on Basu's arm. He brushed it off without thinking and jarred Aryabhata's hand, which skidded across the ink. Aryabhata looked up in a flash of anger and thundered, "Who are you?"

"I am just a merchant's son," confessed Basu, "but I've come here desperate to benefit from your knowledge and hoping to absorb a fraction of your wisdom."

Aryabhata fixed him with a hard stare and replied grudgingly, "All right. You may ask me one question."

Basu thought for a long moment. "I walked 50,348 steps to get here, and then crossed your courtyard, cutting it in half, in half again, and again. Now our arms have brushed, and I cannot get any closer, but I am lost because I have no number to tell me the distance between us. What is the number that tells how many steps I have to go?"

A broad smile lit Aryabhata's face. "You have just asked the very question I have been working on for many moons. The answer is *zero*. There are zero steps left. Zero is the number."

"There's one other thing I want to know—" Basu began.

Aryabhata interrupted. "You have zero questions left!" he admonished. Basu looked crushed with disappointment, but Aryabhata laughed. "Zero, plus one thousand! You may ask me as many questions as you wish, because I think we can learn a lot together."

Name _____

A. Reread the passage and answer the questions.

1. What details from the first paragraph help you determine this story's point of view?

   _____

   _____

   _____

2. At the beginning of paragraph 5, what does the narrator say about Aryabhata's thoughts?

   _____

   _____

3. Is the person telling the story a character in the story? How do you know?

   _____

   _____

   _____

4. What is the point of view of this story?

   _____

B. Work with a partner. Read the passage aloud. Pay attention to expression. Stop after one minute. Fill out the chart.

	Words Read	–	Number of Errors	=	Words Correct Score
First Read		–		=	
Second Read		–		=	

Name _____

Urco: Craftsman in Training

"Father, I am meant to be a craftsman, an artist," pleaded Urco, a twelve-year-old Inca boy. The year was 1425.

"No, I absolutely refuse. You must work as a laborer like the rest of us, building roads, fortresses, and temples in our great city of Cuzco," replied Urco's father. As angry as he felt toward his father, Urco knew that most Inca men did exactly what his father described. They dedicated their lives to building the city, which was high in the mountains. Urco, however, was different. He wanted to create golden goblets and ornaments for the nobles and the emperor! Now, Urco had to convince his father to agree.

Answer the questions about the text.

1. What is the time and place of this historical fiction?

   _____

   _____

2. What does the text tell you about life during the time of the Incas?

   _____

   _____

3. Give an example of dialogue from the text and explain how it helps you learn about the character.

   _____

   _____

   _____

Name _____

**Read each excerpt from the passage and the meaning of the
suffix of the word in bold. Then write a possible meaning for
the word in bold.**

1. Basu counted the steps, doing quick **measurements** as he
   walked along the south bank of India's Ganges River, kicking
   up the hot, dusty ground.
   –ment means "act of" or "state of"

   _____

2. According to the local scholars, the book described the earth as a
   sphere that rotated around the sun, and it explained mathematics,
   time, **astronomy**, and other mysteries of the universe.
   -nomy means "law"

   _____

3. Basu dragged a stick along the dirt, drawing a line. Was it a
   straight line between where he just was and where he was going?
   He posed **question** after question to himself to pass the time.
   –tion means "state of"

   _____

4. Basu was so close, he could see the **mysterious** numbers
   and symbols.
   –ous means "full of" or "having"

   _____

5. Basu looked crushed with **disappointment**, but Aryabhata
   laughed.
   –ment means "act of" or "state of"

   _____

Name _____

voter	brutal	favor	focus	vital

A. Read each word below. Choose a word from the box that rhymes with it and write the word on the line. Then underline the open syllable in both words.

1. futile _____

2. flavor _____

3. crocus _____

4. tidal _____

5. motor _____

B. Read each sentence. Circle the two-syllable word with an open syllable.

6. My soccer shorts are made of nylon.

7. How can you resist a picnic on a warm day?

8. The football team plays its rival on Saturday.

9. It is brave to stand on stage and recite poetry.

10. My dad could detect the smell of onions in the house.

Name _____

A. Read the draft model. Use the questions that follow the draft to help you think about transitions to clarify shifts in time or setting.

Draft Model

Uncle Max agreed to show me the magic trick. I tried to learn how to hold the coin the way he showed me. I got it, and I pulled the coin out of Uncle Max's ear.

---

1. When and why did Uncle Max agree to teach the narrator the trick?

2. What happened after Uncle Max agreed? How was the narrator able to learn to do the trick?

3. What transitional words and phrases could be added to help connect all the events?

B. Now revise the draft by adding transitions to clarify shifts in time or setting.

_____

_____

_____

_____

_____

_____

Name _____

The student who wrote the paragraphs below used text evidence from two different sources to respond to the prompt: *Write a short narrative from Min's point of view as he decides to trust Tree-Ear and offers to teach him.*

Over the next few days, I noticed that Tree-Ear worked hard and did not speak other than saying, "Good morning" at the beginning of the day and, "Thank you for this opportunity, honorable sir" at the end of the day. I was impressed. I remembered what the boy had said about watching me work. I also remembered that I would not be the great potter I was if it weren't for my grandfather, who taught me.

"What does your father do?" I asked the boy the next day. When I heard the boy's story about being an orphan and living with Crane-Man under the bridge, my heart softened. Again I watched the tattered boy finish another day of hard work. After Tree-Ear left, I sat in my workshop, thinking. I thought, "Everyone who has a desire to create pottery should be able to learn. Tree-Ear is honest and willing to work hard."

So the next morning, when Tree-Ear said, "Good morning," I smiled and greeted the boy with a slab of clay.

"Today you will not work," I said. "Today you will learn."

Reread the passage. Follow the directions below.

1. From whose point of view is this sample written? **Circle** a word or words that the show the point of view.

2. **Underline** descriptive details that help the reader picture what is being described.

3. **Draw a box** around a transition that tells when a scene takes place.

4. **Write** a possessive noun on the line.

_____

Name _____

> commemorate   forlorn   contemplate   majestic

Finish each sentence using the vocabulary word provided.

1. **(majestic)** During our travels, _____

_____ .

2. **(forlorn)** The lost dog had _____

_____ .

3. **(commemorate)** On the Fourth of July _____

_____ .

4. **(contemplate)** Before responding to an important question, _____

_____ .

Name _____

Read the selection. Complete the theme graphic organizer.

Detail

↓

Detail

↓

Detail

↓

Theme

Name _____

Read the passage. Check your understanding by asking yourself what the message of the poem is.

At Grandmother's Pueblo

When I visit my grandmother's pueblo,
6 | I hear songs I can't understand.
12 | I see folks who are happy and smiling
20 | Saying welcome to family land.

25 | New Mexico, so dry and vast,
31 | Holds a painted canvas before me,
37 | With deserts and valleys and mountains
43 | As far as the eye can see.

50 | Nature proudly displays
53 | Her work for us to savor.
59 | When the sun bows low, I see
66 | A rainbow like a party favor.

72 | Grandmother weaves her blankets
76 | And tells us stories of tricksters.
82 | I listen as if in a trance
89 | While the campfire dances and flickers.

95 | When Grandma comes to my room
101 | Later on, she holds to the light
108 | A blanket she made just for me
115 | That holds me in its arms all night.

Name _____

A. Reread the passage and answer the questions.

1. What do the words in line 2—"I hear songs I can't understand"—tell you about the speaker's experience at the grandmother's pueblo?

   _____

   _____

2. Based on the speaker's descriptions in stanzas 2, 3, and 4, how do you think the speaker feels about being at the pueblo?

   _____

   _____

3. How does the speaker describe the blanket from Grandma? How does the blanket make the speaker feel?

   _____

   _____

4. Based on the details and descriptions, what do you think is the theme of this poem?

   _____

   _____

B. Work with a partner. Read the passage aloud. Pay attention to expression and phrasing. Stop after one minute. Fill out the chart.

	Words Read	–	Number of Errors	=	Words Correct Score
First Read		–		=	
Second Read		–		=	

Name _____

Museum Trip

While walking through the gallery, it seemed
That I was on a journey through the years.
Ancient statues stared ahead and dreamed.
Waiting, watching, beckoning each appeared.
Look at these and this and those things, they said,
As I saw the cases of golden things
That were useful to people so long dead,
Golden crowns and cups, masks and bowls and rings.
But then the afternoon grew late, and we
Had to leave this place of treasures and things rare.
And though we left there's so much more to see.
I want to come back here again to share.
It makes me wonder what on Earth they'd say
If those people were here to tell us today.

Answer the questions about the text.

1. How do you know this is a lyric poem? How do you know it is a sonnet?

   _____

   _____

   _____

   _____

2. Copy one line of the poem. Then place an accent mark above each stressed syllable.

   _____

3. Write an example from the poem of four words that create a rhyme scheme.

   _____

Name _____

> **Rhyme scheme** is a pattern of rhyming words at the ends of lines.
>
> **Meter** is a pattern of stressed and unstressed syllables.
>
> Rhyme scheme and meter give poetry a lyrical, musical quality.

Read the stanza from a lyric poem below. Then answer the questions.

At Grandmother's Pueblo

Nature proudly displays
Her work for us to savor.
When the sun bows low, I see
A rainbow like a party favor.

1. Going from top to bottom, assign a letter—*a, b, c, d*—to each *new* sound at the end of a line. If a sound rhymes with an earlier one, give it the same letter as the rhyming word. If not, give it a new letter. Write the rhyme scheme of the stanza.

   _____

2. Which syllables in each line need to be stressed? Write the last line of the stanza on the line below. Underline each syllable that needs to be stressed.

   _____

3. How do you think rhyme and meter affect this poem?

   _____

   _____

4. Write a short poem about one of your favorite places. Write one four-line stanza. Use an *abcb* rhyme scheme and a meter of your choice.

   _____

   _____

   _____

Name _____

Read each passage. Then answer the questions about personification.

1. New Mexico, so dry and vast,
    holds a painted canvas before me

    What is personified? _____

    What is its human action? _____

2. Nature proudly displays
    Her work for us to savor.

    What is personified? _____

    What is its human action? _____

3. When the sun bows low, I see
    A rainbow like a party favor.

    What is personified? _____

    What is its human action? _____

4. I listen as if in a trance
    While the campfire dances and flickers.

    What is personified? _____

    What is its human action? _____

5. A blanket she made just for me
    That holds me in its arms all night.

    What is personified? _____

    What is its human action? _____

Name _____

throttling	squiggle	befuddle	scramble	simplicity
noodle	scrambling	simple	throttle	squiggly

A. Read the first syllables below. Then write the word from the box that begins with the first syllable and ends with a consonant + *le* **syllable.**

1. throt-   _____

2. scram-   _____

3. squig-   _____

4. noo-   _____

5. sim-   _____

B. Read each sentence. Circle the word that has a consonant + *le* **final syllable. Then write the consonant +** *le* **syllable on the line.**

6. Their squabble did not interrupt the dinner. _____

7. Our beagle has been trained to fetch a ball. _____

8. We enjoyed hearing the sound of the train whistle. _____

9. I ride my bicycle to school every day. _____

10. The ice skater performed a quadruple jump. _____

Name _____

A. Read the draft model. Use the questions that follow the draft to help you think of precise, vivid words you can add.

Draft Model

Wherever I go, I bring my sketchpad and special pencil. They are two of my favorite possessions. The pages are blank until I draw a picture on them. This is why I love my sketchbook so much.

---

1. What does the sketchbook look like? Why is the pencil special?

2. What descriptive words can show how the narrator feels about the blank pages?

3. What precise, vivid words can describe the drawings the narrator creates on the sketchbook pages?

B. Now revise the draft by adding precise, vivid words to help readers understand more about the writer and the sketchbook.

_____

_____

_____

_____

_____

_____

_____

_____

_____

_____

Name _____

The student who wrote the poem below used two different sources to respond to the prompt: *Write a lyric poem about a family tradition.*

If Grandma's kitchen table could talk,
It would have many stories to tell.
Because unlike other kitchen tables,
It's had generations to dwell
On the laughter, tears, and secrets
Shared around its oval, wooden top.
From Happy Birthdays to new siblings—
It's the only unchanged prop
In the photos I see now.
There it is in black and white.
My mom, the birthday girl, turned one.

It held Grandma's "Celebration Cake."
Wow, Grandma sure looked young!

It's held all our Celebration Cakes
And heard all our birthday wishes.
And it's always waited patiently
While we helped clear all the dishes.

I love Grandma's kitchen table.
It's where my family comes together.
And there's one thing I know for sure—
It will save our stories forever.

Reread the passage. Follow the directions below.

1. From whose point of view is this poem written? **Circle** words that reveal the narrator.

2. **Underline** precise language that helps the reader picture what is being described.

3. **Draw a box** around a transition that tells when a scene takes place.

4. **Write** an appositive on the line.

_____

Name _____

resemblance	unseemly	enthralled	regulation
capacity	fallow	negotiate	insight

Use each pair of vocabulary words in a single sentence.

1. enthralled, resemblance

_____

_____

2. unseemly, negotiate

_____

_____

3. capacity, regulation

_____

_____

4. fallow, insight

_____

_____

Name _____

Read the selection. Complete the theme graphic organizer.

> **Detail**

⬇

> **Detail**

⬇

> **Detail**

⬇

> **Theme**

Name _____

Read the passage. Use the make, confirm, and revise predictions strategy to help you understand the theme.

Stuck Together

13	Rosa entered her apartment building just as a woman with red hair was coming out. The woman nodded at Rosa but didn't say anything. Rosa
25	
37	remembered seeing the woman when she was getting mail, but other than that, Rosa had no idea who she was. Then again, Rosa didn't know anyone
51	in the building. She and her mother had just moved in a month ago, and
66	while people weren't rude, they weren't exactly friendly, either. Everyone
76	kept to himself or herself. Rosa missed the people in her old building
89	where tenants knew one another and chatted in the lobby, knocked on
101	doors to borrow milk, and had a big holiday party annually.
112	Rosa pushed the "up" button on the elevator and allowed her backpack
124	to drop to the floor as she waited for the elevator to arrive. And waited.
139	And then she waited some more. "Oh no," she muttered quietly to herself,
152	"not again."
154	Rosa lived on the seventh floor. Sighing, she slung the strap of her
167	heavy backpack over her shoulder and trudged slowly up the stairs. By the
180	time she got to her floor, there were beads of sweat rolling down her face.
195	Rosa's mother was inside the apartment, painting the walls. "Que pasa,
206	mija?" asked her mother.
210	"I had to walk up the stairs, again. Somebody should do something
222	about that elevator," Rosa answered.
227	"I called the landlord several times, but I haven't heard anything back,"
239	her mother told her.
243	The next morning, Rosa and her mother walked to the elevator and
255	hoped for the best. Luckily, the elevator actually arrived. There were a
267	few people already on it, including the red-haired lady. Rosa and her
279	mother entered, and the doors closed behind them. People smiled, but
290	no one spoke. That is, nobody spoke until they realized that the elevator
303	wasn't moving.
305	"Great," the woman with the red hair said sarcastically.

"I've written to the landlord about how frequently this broken elevator malfunctions," said a man with a black briefcase. He pulled the red alarm button, and it began to clang outside the door. "Now we just have to wait until someone hears the signal and pushes a button for the elevator."

Rosa looked at her mom, who smiled and said, "It doesn't seem like the landlord is listening to our complaints. Maybe if we all got together and pressured him, he would fix the elevator."

"I don't know," said a man in jogging shorts. "I don't really like to get involved in problems."

Rosa smiled at him. "You're stuck in an elevator. You're already involved." She put out her hand. "I'm Rosa, in 7L, and this is my mom, Maria."

The man shook Rosa's hand. "Okay, you have a point. I'm Saul, 8R."

One by one, everyone in the elevator introduced himself or herself, and as they waited, they talked about the difficulties they'd been having with the elevator and ways to get the landlord to fix it.

"Perhaps if we could write a letter and have everyone in the building sign it, the landlord would listen," someone suggested.

"We could say that we are going to contact the city's housing department," Saul put in. "Or if we all say that we won't pay our rent, I bet we get the elevator fixed."

"I can write the letter," offered Rosa's mother.

The other people in the elevator agreed to review the letter and help get signatures from all the building's tenants.

Just then the elevator started descending again. As it made its way down to the first floor, Rosa felt proud of her mother for getting everyone to agree to work together. Maybe this building would turn out to be as friendly as the old one. At the very least, it would have a working elevator.

Name _____

A. Reread the passage and answer the questions.

1. At the beginning of the story, how does Rosa feel about living in her new building?

   _____

   _____

2. What had happened when Rosa's mother called the landlord about the broken elevator?

   _____

3. How do the people in the elevator respond when Rosa's mother says they should get together and pressure the landlord to fix the elevator?

   _____

   _____

   _____

4. Based on the events of the story, what do you think the theme of this story is?

   _____

   _____

B. Work with a partner. Read the passage aloud. Pay attention to expression. Stop after one minute. Fill out the chart.

	Words Read	–	Number of Errors	=	Words Correct Score
First Read		–		=	
Second Read		–		=	

Name _____

Practice Makes Perfect

    "Rosa, it's a great way to practice your Italian," my mother had told me. She had asked me to babysit for Christina, my four-year-old cousin from Italy.

    "La palla!" Christina screams from the backyard.

    "What are you saying?" I mumble. Crying, she points up at a red ball caught in the tree.

    My neighbors, the Chens, rush over. "Why is Christina screaming?" they ask. "Her ball's up there," I reply.

    "Get some other balls from the bin, Rosa," Mrs. Chen suggests. "We'll toss them up and try to free hers."

    Agreeing, we throw balls into the tree, knocking the red one down. "La palla," I say, handing Christina her ball.

    Mr. Chen says, "Rosa, you speak Italian!"

Answer the questions about the text.

1. List three text features that let you know this is realistic fiction.

   _____

   _____

2. From what point of view is the story told? How do you know?

   _____

   _____

3. How is foreign language dialogue used to portray Christina?

   _____

   _____

4. How does the first sentence of the text foreshadow future events?

   _____

   _____

   _____

Name _____

In each item below, underline the context clues that help define the word in bold. Then write the word's meaning on the line.

1. Rosa missed the people in her old building where **tenants** knew one another and chatted in the lobby, knocked on doors to borrow milk, and had a big holiday party annually.

   _____

2. "Oh no," she **muttered** quietly to herself, "not again."

   _____

3. Sighing, she **slung** the strap of her heavy backpack over her shoulder and trudged slowly up the stairs.

   _____

4. Sighing, she slung the strap of her backpack over her shoulder and **trudged** slowly up the stairs. By the time she got to her floor, there were beads of sweat rolling down her face.

   _____

5. "I've written to the landlord about how frequently this broken elevator **malfunctions**," said a man with a black briefcase.

   _____

6. Just then the elevator started **descending** again. As it made its way down to the first floor, Rosa felt proud of her mother for getting everyone to agree to work together.

   _____

Name _____

A. Read each word below and listen for the sound of the vowel team. Sort the words by writing them in the correct column below. Underline the vowel team in each word.

| moisten | guarantee | household | impeach | exploit |
| painful | agreed | straighten | about | creatures |

ai as in *main*	*ea* as in *reader*	*ee* as in *breezy*	*ou* as in *mouth*	*oi* as in *coil*
_____	_____	_____	_____	_____
_____	_____	_____	_____	_____

B. Find the word in each row that has a vowel team used in the chart above. Write the word on the line, divide the word into syllables, and circle the vowel team.

1. streamline   shimmer   solution   _____

2. calming   earthbound   coward   _____

3. equality   pedigree   understood   _____

4. spoilage   paper   lurking   _____

5. education   boyhood   gaining   _____

Name_____

A. Read the draft model. Use the questions that follow the draft to help you think about transitional words and phrases that will make it easier for readers to keep track of where and when events take place.

Draft Model

It had snowed hard during the night. The snow was very deep. Sally and her sisters built a snow fort. They saw that their elderly neighbors needed help shoveling their sidewalk. Sally and her sisters discussed together the idea of helping them.

---

1. What transitional words and phrases would show when Sally and her sisters built the fort? What words and phrases would show when other events happened?

2. What transitional words and phrases would show where different events took place?

3. What other words and phrases would help guide the reader smoothly from one event to the next?

B. Now revise the draft by adding transitions to help readers keep track of when events take place and where the sisters are when events occur.

_____

_____

_____

_____

_____

_____

Name _____

The student who wrote the paragraphs below used relevant details from two different sources to respond to the prompt: *Imagine that Tía Lola visited the castle and solved the king's problem. Write a scene in which Tía Lola talks to the musicians and solves the king's problem.*

When Tía Lola entered the courtyard, she saw that the musicians were just as disappointed as the king. They slumped in their chairs, like a defeated sports team. Tía Lola decided to give the musicians a pep talk. "Hola!" she said. "I heard each of you play for the king. You are all very talented!" Most of the musicians sat up a little straighter, but the violinist crossed his arms.

"Then why isn't the king satisfied?" he asked.

"Well," explained Tía Lola, "The king's servant told me that the king missed the chorus of birds that sing together in the summer. Each bird sang a different song, but hearing their combined songs made the king happy."

The musicians listened, so Tía Lola continued. "You have brought music from all over the world, and while each of your songs is impressive, just think how beautiful it would sound if you all shared your music and played together!"

All of the musicians—including the violinist—agreed, and began to play together. The king heard the music and smiled.

Reread the passage. Follow the directions below.

1. Where does Tía Lola talk to the musicians? **Circle** the transitional phrase that shows where this scene takes place.

2. **Draw a box** around the relevant details that show why the king was disappointed.

3. **Underline** the dialogue that shows how Tía Lola solved the king's problem.

4. **Write** one of the action verbs on the line.

    _____

Name _____

recoiled	feebly	skewed	roused
vastness	summon	persistent	dilemma

Finish each sentence using the vocabulary word provided.

1. **(summon)** In order to lift the heavy box, _____

_____ .

2. **(feebly)** The sick dog _____

_____ .

3. **(dilemma)** Having to decide _____

_____ .

4. **(roused)** This morning, my parents _____

_____ .

5. **(vastness)** After our ship left the port, _____

_____ .

6. **(recoiled)** The boy _____

_____ .

7. **(persistent)** In order to get this problem solved _____

_____ .

8. **(skewed)** The path of the storm suddenly _____

_____ .

Name _____

Read the selection. Complete the theme graphic organizer.

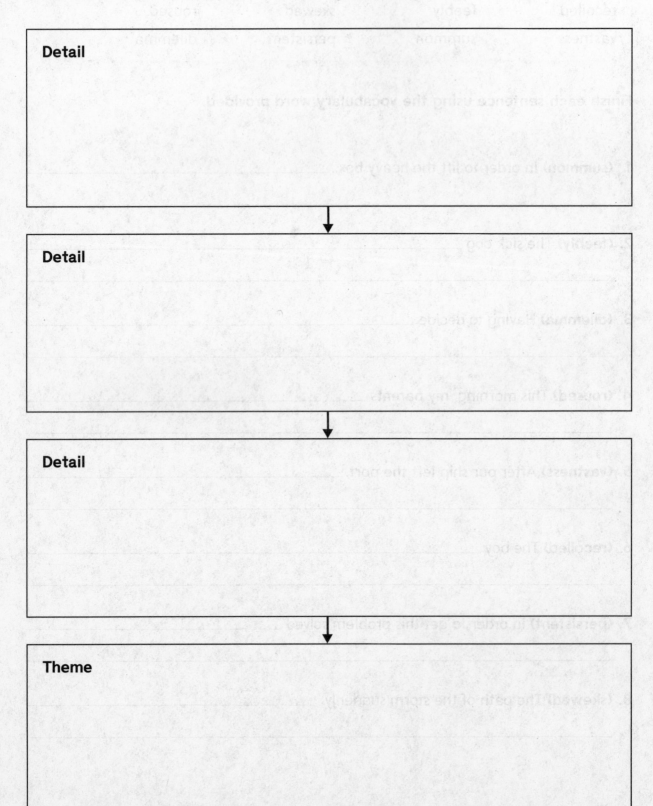

Detail

Detail

Detail

Theme

Name _____

Read the passage. Use the make, confirm, and revise predictions strategy to help you understand the theme.

Poppy and the Junior Tigers

8	Poppy observed the group of 12-year-olds listlessly dribbling basketballs around the court at the community center.
16	"C'mon," Poppy shouted. "More energy! Try passing." As usual,
25	however, passing was a total disaster. Balls hit people's heads, legs, and
37	shoulders and only very occasionally landed in anyone's hands.
46	Poppy shook her head in disbelief. This was not what she had had in
60	mind when she had volunteered to coach the community junior league
71	basketball team. She had figured she'd be a superb basketball coach. After
83	all, she was a state champion forward on her high school's basketball
95	team. Coaching would be fun! But after a few weeks with the Junior
108	Tigers, Poppy was changing her tune. Not only were the Junior Tigers not
121	interested in dribbling drills, but they also balked at running drills and
133	shooting drills. Although Poppy had tried to explain just how important the
145	drills were to performing well, the Junior Tigers just didn't appear to care.
158	Poppy called out, "Kia, you're begging for someone to steal the ball.
170	Pass lower! Rosa, stop fiddling with your hair and focus! Carl, don't run
183	with the ball, but don't trip over it, either."
192	Mike, a tall, skinny kid who enjoyed hogging the ball, smirked. "Yeah,
204	Carl, love your coordination."
208	"Cut it out, Mike," said Poppy. "Can we please actually function like a
221	team?"
222	That evening, Poppy explained the situation to her dad. "None of the
234	children seem to care about playing well, and I just don't see the point
248	when they make no effort. Maybe I should just quit and put us all out of
264	our misery."

Name _____

"Or maybe they just need some really compelling motivation," said Poppy's dad.

The following day at practice, Poppy made an announcement to the team. "You know, you guys could be playing games that make your community proud. You could be learning teamwork and cooperation skills that will help you your whole life, and some of you could maybe be good enough to one day get a basketball scholarship. Instead, you just want to fool around. You don't care, and since you don't care, well, I don't care either. So, I want to tell you that today is my last day coaching you guys. Oh, and yeah, by the way, the center has to find a replacement, and unless that happens, it will be your last week for a while, as well."

"Really?" asked Mike, looking crestfallen, his usual grin gone. "But I like basketball."

"Yeah, we all do. Don't you think you're being a little mean?" asked Kia. "We're just kids."

Poppy sighed, "Yep, kids that should try harder and put in real effort. Now, line up for layups. I'm still the coach for now."

To Poppy's surprise, the Junior Tigers actually lined up without the usual shoving and pushing. They took turns shooting at the basket in an almost orderly fashion, and when Carl missed, Mike did not make fun of him.

Poppy tried dribbling drills. While there was still a bit too much chatter and running with the ball, for once, there was no loud complaining.

At the end of practice, Poppy felt encouraged. She said, "Hey, guys! You made some effort out there, so I'll make some effort as well. If you want to do this—really do this the right way—I'll stick around and try to whip you into shape. What do you think? Raise your hand if you are really ready to be a team."

Then Poppy smiled because everyone's hand went up.

Name _____

A. Reread the passage and answer the questions.

1. In the beginning of the passage, how does Poppy feel about the Junior Tigers? Why?

   _____

   _____

2. What does Poppy need to do to get the team to work harder in practice?

   _____

3. How do the Junior Tigers change their behavior when they think Poppy is going to quit?

   _____

   _____

4. What do you think the theme of this story is?

   _____

   _____

B. Work with a partner. Read the passage aloud. Pay attention to phrasing. Stop after one minute. Fill out the chart.

	Words Read	–	Number of Errors	=	Words Correct Score
First Read		–		=	
Second Read		–		=	

Name _____

Mustering Courage

On weekends, Julian toils hard at his landscaping job, mowing lawns, clipping hedges, and heaving heavy loads of mulch all morning. By noon, he is starving, so he heads toward the town deli to buy lunch. A long line confronts him, and his stomach growls angrily. "Who's next? What can I get for you?" the man at the deli counter hollers.

People behind Julian start to shout their orders: "Tuna on whole wheat!" "Hot pastrami on rye!" "Grilled cheese!" Julian gazes around and feels lost. His English is improving, but at times his throat closes and his face reddens.

A woman says to him, "It's your turn, dear. Go ahead. I will wait."

Julian musters his courage. "Turkey on a roll!" he shouts.

"You got it, my friend," answers the man.

Confident, Julian replies, "Thanks, buddy!"

Answer the questions about the text.

1. List three text features that let you know this is realistic fiction.

_____

_____

2. From what point of view is the story told? How do you know?

_____

_____

3. Choose a sentence from the text that contains strong verbs. How does this sentence provide a vivid picture?

_____

_____

4. What is the theme of the story? List one clue that the writer provides.

_____

_____

_____

Name _____

Read each passage. Underline the context clues that help you figure out the meaning of each word in bold. Then write the word's meaning on the line.

1. Not only were the Junior Tigers not interested in dribbling drills, but they also **balked** at running drills and shooting drills. Although Poppy had tried to explain just how important the drills were to performing well, the Junior Tigers just didn't appear to care.

   _____

2. Poppy called out, "Kia, you're begging for someone to steal the ball. Pass lower! Rosa, stop **fiddling** with your hair and focus!"

   _____

3. "Really?" asked Mike, looking **crestfallen,** his usual grin gone. "But I like basketball."

   _____

4. "Carl, don't run with the ball, but don't trip over it, either." Mike, a tall, skinny kid who enjoyed hogging the ball, smirked. "Yeah, Carl, love your **coordination.**"

   _____

5. To Poppy's surprise, the Junior Tigers actually lined up without the usual shoving and pushing. They took turns shooting at the basket in an almost orderly **fashion.**

   _____

Name _____

A. Read each sentence. Circle the word with an *r*-controlled vowel syllable. Write the word on the line and underline the *r*-controlled vowel syllable.

1. I am the only daughter in my family. _____

2. My ancestors came to the United States from China. _____

3. Would you like oil and vinegar dressing on your salad? _____

4. I like to keep a calendar in my notebook. _____

5. The class chose apple juice as its top flavor. _____

6. My dad made a huge vegetable platter for the holiday. _____

B. Read the words in the box below. Sort the words by their *r*-controlled vowel syllable. Write the words that have the same final syllable in the correct column.

cellar	observer	janitor	traitor
waiter	singular	customer	similar
actor	dollar	ancestor	stroller

-er	*-tor*	*-lar*
_____	_____	_____
_____	_____	_____
_____	_____	_____

Name _____

A. Read the draft model. Use the questions that follow the draft to help you think of ways to make the conclusion stronger.

Draft Model

Susan said her last lines in the play and the stage went dark. The lights came back on, and the audience went wild with applause. She had done it!

---

1. How does Susan feel when she hears the audience's reaction? Why?

2. What does Susan learn about herself from finishing the performance?

3. What other details could help clarify previous events and give readers a sense of closure?

B. Now revise the draft by adding details that will help the reader better understand how Susan feels and what she has learned.

_____

_____

_____

_____

_____

_____

_____

The student who wrote the paragraphs below used details from two different sources to respond to the prompt: *Rewrite the scene in "Confronting a Challenge" where the narrator discovers the pond and the two skaters. Include descriptive details of the setting and dialogue in the new scene.*

One day I walked a different route home from school. The path I chose led to an open field and allowed me to really see the sky. It was pure blue except for a few cloudy wisps and a thin, white trail of a faraway jet. I had to take my eyes off of the sky to watch my step, though, because the ground began to feel uneven. Before I knew it, I was going down a small hill. At the bottom I found a large pond that was completely frozen over.

There, a woman and a young girl were skating. I was too embarrassed to ask Ben for help, but this woman was a stranger. I could ask her. I walked down to the edge of the pond. "Excuse me," I said, "I just moved from California and I can't skate. Could you teach me?"

"Sure!" But it wasn't the woman who answered. It was the girl. She sped over and skid to a stop. "I'll teach you how to skate like a pro."

Reread the passage. Follow the directions below.

1. **Circle** descriptive details that help develop the scene.

2. **Draw a box** around the relevant details that reveal the narrator's problem.

3. **Underline** the dialogue that shows how the narrator's problem will be solved in this new scene.

4. **Write** one of the past-tense verbs on the line.

_____

Name _____

> windswept   sharecropper   impoverished   abundant
>
> unearthed   solitude   ingenuity   productivity

Use each pair of vocabulary words in a single sentence.

1. sharecropper, windswept

_____

_____

2. impoverished, unearthed

_____

_____

3. ingenuity, productivity

_____

_____

4. abundant, solitude

_____

_____

Name _____

Read the selection. Complete the sequence graphic organizer.

Event

Name _____

Read the passage. Use the summarize strategy to identify important ideas and events.

Clean Water Partners

	The facts are clear. Nearly a billion people in the world need safer
13	drinking water. Unclean water causes many diseases that result in millions
24	of deaths. Imagine how your life would be transformed if you didn't have
37	a reliable supply of water. What if your water was contaminated?
48	**A Water Crisis**
51	In some countries, people spend hours a day carrying water to their
63	homes. Women and girls are often the ones assigned the chore of collecting
76	water. Because of this chore, the women cannot take jobs, which would help
89	their finances. The girls are unable to attend school, which would prepare
101	them for future opportunities. Sometimes they must walk long distances to
112	find water, but often the water is unhealthy. Where water is scarce, people
125	are usually poor. Where there is no clean water, people are often sick.
138	**Solving the Problem**
141	Getting clean water to all people is a serious problem. However, some
153	progress has been made. More people are speaking out, drawing attention to
165	this concern. Many groups are actively raising money to build wells in remote
178	places. People are working together to provide clean water for those in need.
191	**First Things First**
194	To start a water project, planners know what must come first. Outsiders
206	must take time to learn the beliefs and culture of the people they want to
221	help. Once there is trust and respect, then everyone can begin working
233	together to solve the problem.
238	The next step is to train members of the community. Project planners teach
251	people how the water source will work. The people can learn about sanitation
264	issues. They discover how to troubleshoot problems that may arise later. When
276	everyone agrees on the plan, then the community decides how to participate.

Name_____

Everybody Worked Together

Modderspruit is a tiny village in South Africa. They had nothing but a trickle of water for nearly 2,000 families. The villagers knew they must act to solve their problem. A dam had been built in the region in the 1920s, creating a reservoir. It was used mostly to water farm crops. Over the years, more and more canals were added like fingers on a hand. Those canals distributed water to new villages. Over time, the people who lived at the end of the line had little or no water.

The village of Modderspruit is about an hour's drive from Johannesburg, the capital of Gauteng, a province of South Africa.

To survive, the villagers had to transport water from a water source across a busy highway. Every day they dodged speeding vehicles as they carried containers of water to their homes. Even the highway company recognized the villagers' need.

Teamwork

In a spirit of cooperation, the highway owners offered to help. They promised to drill a borehole, a deep hole used to find a hidden source of water. The villagers had a community center that was seldom used because there was no water for it. Modderspruit decided the center would be a perfect location to drill.

Then the highway company contacted another agency to help with the next step. Once the water was found, it had to get above ground to the people. It was time to decide how to pump the water to the community center. The agency and village leaders decided on a solar-powered pump. There is only a little electricity in South Africa but a lot of sunshine. A solar pump and two 5,000-liter storage tanks were installed at the center. The borehole successfully produced an abundance of clean water.

A Satisfying Outcome

The villagers often use the community center now. Water is available for bathrooms and showers. The children can play and attend school instead of always carrying water. The villagers are grateful for all the people who helped solve their problem.

Name _____

A. Reread the passage and answer the questions.

1. What is the main problem mentioned in the first paragraph?

_____

2. List the events under the heading "Teamwork" that helped the villagers of Modderspruit, South Africa, build a new well.

_____

_____

_____

_____

_____

3. What was the outcome of the steps used to solve the village's water problem?

_____

_____

_____

B. Work with a partner. Read the passage aloud. Pay attention to rate and accuracy. Stop after one minute. Fill out the chart.

	Words Read	–	Number of Errors	=	Words Correct Score
First Read		–		=	
Second Read		–		=	

Name _____

Florida Community Defeats Air Polluters

For 30 years, a charcoal factory owned by Royal Oak Corporation operated in Ocala, Florida. Ruth Reed, a community leader of African American homeowners, organized her neighbors to demand that the factory stop polluting the air. The group wrote letters to city and state officials to complain. When that didn't work, they hung bed sheets out to catch soot from the factory and brought the dirty sheets to city council meetings as proof. Eventually, government agencies listened and said they would investigate. Not trusting them, Ruth's group wisely hired their own experts to test the air. Afraid of what the tests would reveal, Royal Oak decided to close the factory.

Answer the questions about the text.

1. What two features of narrative nonfiction can you find in this text?

   _____

   _____

   _____

2. What is the text's topic? What was your first clue?

   _____

   _____

3. Give an example of a sentence in the text that shows the author's tone and point of view on the topic.

   _____

   _____

4. List two important facts from the text that are important to the story.

   _____

   _____

Name _____

A. Choose the prefix *un-* or *trans-* to change the meaning of each word below. Then use each word in a sentence.

1. **clean** _____

_____

2. **helpful** _____

_____

3. **form** _____

_____

4. **port** _____

_____

5. **available** _____

_____

B. Read the words below. On the line provided write how (or whether) the part of speech changes when the suffix changes.

6. sanitary ⟶ sanitation

_____

7. transport ⟶ transportation

_____

8. plan ⟶ planner

_____

9. outside ⟶ outsiders

_____

Name _____

dollar	people	enough	answer	address
instead	receive	children	always	receipt

A. Read the words in the box above. On the lines below, write the words that have two syllables that are divided between consonants. Mark the other words with an X.

_____   _____   _____

_____   _____   _____

B. In each row, choose the word with a vowel team that makes the short vowel sound in bold. Write the word. Then underline the two letters that make the vowel team.

1. **short e**   against   strain   retrieve   _____

2. **short e**   believe   railroad   ready   _____

3. **short e**   greed   guess   monkey   _____

4. **short u**   enough   cloud   scream   _____

5. **short u**   cousin   coarse   tiptoe   _____

6. **short u**   refuse   boast   because   _____

Name _____

A. Read the draft model. Use the questions that follow the draft to help you think about what relevant details and evidence you can add.

Draft Model

Mom and Dad were tired because they had three kids and full-time jobs. I got my big brothers to agree that we would cook dinner twice a week. Everything is better now.

---

1. What facts, examples, or quotations could you add to help readers understand the family's situation?

2. What details could you add to help readers understand the narrator's actions?

3. What details would help readers better understand and visualize the conclusion?

B. Now revise the draft by adding relevant details and evidence to help readers learn more about how one family solves a problem.

_____

_____

_____

_____

_____

_____

_____

Name _____

The student who wrote the paragraphs below used text evidence from two different sources to answer the question: *How can culture improve a community?*

Culture is an important part of a community—it can even improve a community. For example, the village where Juan Quezada lived used to be poor. People worked hard for very little money. When Juan discovered the pottery-making process of the Casas Grandes people, however, things began to change. Juan used resources from the land to make pottery the same way the Casas Grandes people made it 600 years earlier. He taught his family and friends how to make the pottery, too. Now, people his village are working successfully as artists.

Kids can realize the importance of culture in a community, too. For example, in "A Box of Ideas," Ms. Cerda told the students about a tradition of making nichos, which are homemade boxes that symbolize important aspects of a family or community. The students made their own nichos and sold them to make money to improve the school library.

Both the pottery and nichos originated from traditions of a culture. People worked together and used resources around the communities to improve their communities.

Reread the passage. Follow the directions below.

1. **Circle** the thesis statement that introduces the topic.

2. **Draw a box** around the relevant details that show how culture can improve a community.

3. **Underline** the conclusion that summarizes how culture can improve a community.

4. **Write** one of the helping verbs followed by a main verb on the line.

_____

Name _____

adept	prominent	spectators	aristocracy
prevail	collective	perseverance	trailblazer

**Write a complete sentence to answer each question below.
In your answer, use the vocabulary word in bold.**

1. What is an activity you want to be more **adept** at doing? _____

_____

2. What might make someone a **prominent** citizen? _____

_____

3. Why would **spectators** go to a basketball game? _____

_____

4. What group of people might be considered part of the **aristocracy**? _____

_____

5. What does it take to **prevail** in a difficult situation? _____

_____

6. What is a **collective** decision? _____

_____

7. Why might someone be considered a **trailblazer**? _____

_____

8. What is an example of **perseverance**? _____

_____

Name _____

Read the selection. Complete the cause and effect graphic organizer.

Cause		Effect
	→	
	→	
	→	
	→	

**Read the passage. Use the summarizing strategy
to identify important events in Clemente's life.**

Roberto Clemente: A Legendary Life

From Puerto Rico to America

5	American Baseball Hall of Famer Roberto Clemente was born in rural
16	Puerto Rico in 1934. No one imagined that little boy would someday set
29	amazing records in baseball. From early childhood, Clemente showed
38	exceptional athletic skill. As a teenager, his passion was baseball.
48	Soon the word was out. Clemente was offered a baseball contract with
60	the Dodgers while he was still in high school. He accepted, but one year
74	later moved on to the Pittsburgh Pirates. Clemente was a Pirate for 18
87	seasons until his untimely death at age 38 in a tragic plane crash.
100	Clemente was an American success story. He rose from a life of poverty
113	to become a professional athlete. He stepped into a sport that had been
126	played mostly by white men. This paved the way for other Latinos.
138	Clemente broke through the racial barriers of his day. To achieve his goals,
151	he overcame many obstacles.

Strike One 155

157	When young Clemente came to the United States, he didn't know
168	English. A worse challenge that he had to face was discrimination.
179	Clemente had not thought much about his race as a black Puerto Rican.
192	However, the United States had laws that separated blacks and whites in
204	the 1950s. Most hotels and restaurants would not allow blacks back then.
216	Clemente had to find separate lodging during spring training. He often ate
228	his meals on the team bus.
234	Clemente may have thrilled baseball fans, but sports reporters did not
245	rally around him. They teased him for his strong Latino accent. Clemente
257	seemed like a foreigner to the African American community. He was
268	an outsider in the mostly white steel town of Pittsburgh. It seemed that
281	Clemente didn't fit in.

Name _____

Clemente quickly became a defender of his rights and the rights of others. When he heard insults thrown at a teammate, Clemente let everyone know it was wrong. He became a leader in the Major League's union. He demanded fair working conditions for all.

Reporters tried to nickname him "Bob" or "Bobby." Clemente rejected those American names. He said words to the effect of "I'm Puerto Rican and you can call me Roberto." He was proud of his heritage.

Play Ball

Clemente was a powerhouse. He was a hard hitter with a lifetime batting average of .317. Clemente routinely kept hopeful batters from getting to base. He could track down balls hit between right and center field with lightning speed. Fans were awed by Clemente's throwing arm.

Clemente won many awards. He took four National League batting titles. Clemente was one of only ten players who had gotten 3,000 base hits. He was awarded 12 Gold Gloves, an honor given to the best fielding players in the league.

Making a Difference

Clemente was a planner and a doer. In 1972 Nicaragua suffered a huge earthquake. Clemente rounded up supplies to aid the victims. On New Year's Eve, he told his wife good-bye and took off on a flight to Nicaragua. Just after the plane was in the air, one of the engines exploded. Then there was another explosion. Two  more blasts followed. The plane went down. When the word got out, fans around the world mourned his death.

Clemente had seen people struggle, and he wanted to help. He died serving others, which had become his life goal. Those who knew him best would say that Clemente was a model of hard work. He was a man of integrity who stood by what he believed.

Clemente was willing to break down barriers and lead the way for others to follow.

Name _____

A. Reread the passage and answer the questions.

1. What were two effects of the discrimination that Clemente faced in the 1950s?

   _____

   _____

   _____

2. What were some effects of Clemente's great skill at playing professional baseball?

   _____

   _____

3. What caused Clemente to travel to Nicaragua in 1972?

   _____

   _____

4. What effect did Clemente's career and life have on Latinos who played professional baseball in later years?

   _____

   _____

B. Work with a partner. Read the passage aloud. Pay attention to phrasing and rate. Stop after one minute. Fill out the chart.

	Words Read	–	Number of Errors	=	Words Correct Score
First Read		–		=	
Second Read		–		=	

Name _____

Thurgood Marshall: First African American Supreme Court Justice

Thurgood Marshall was born on July 2, 1908, in Baltimore, Maryland. After finishing college, he experienced racial discrimination firsthand. He was rejected from University of Maryland law school because he wasn't white. How would this brilliant man resolve this obstacle? He kept his dream and attended Howard University law school. After graduating first in his class from Howard University, Marshall was thinking, "I want to work for the rights of all people," so he became a civil rights lawyer. His biggest victory was Brown *v.* Board of Education of Topeka in 1954. In this case, the Supreme Court found racial segregation in public schools unconstitutional. In 1967 Marshall became the first African American on the Supreme Court. As a Supreme Court Justice, Marshall worked for civil rights until he retired in 1991. He died in 1993.

Answer the questions about the text.

1. How do you know the text is a biography? Who is the subject?

_____

_____

2. What sentence in the text adds suspense and makes you want to know more?

_____

3. What sentence or part of a sentence in the text presents a thought that Marshall may have had?

_____

_____

4. What events do you think caused Marshall to become a civil rights lawyer?

_____

Name _____

**Read each passage. Underline the context clues that help
you figure out the meaning of each word in bold. Then write
the word's meaning on the line.**

1. Clemente was a Pirate for 18 seasons until his **untimely** death
   at age 38 in a tragic plane crash.

   _____

2. Clemente broke through the racial **barriers** of his day. To achieve
   his goals, he overcame many obstacles.

   _____

3. A worse challenge that he had to face was **discrimination**.
   Clemente had not thought much about his race as a black Puerto
   Rican. However, the United States had laws that separated blacks
   and whites in the 1950s. Most hotels and restaurants would not
   allow blacks back then.

   _____

   _____

4. He said words to the effect of "I'm Puerto Rican and you can call
   me Roberto." He was proud of his **heritage**.

   _____

5. Clemente was a **powerhouse**. He was a hard hitter with a lifetime
   batting average of .317. Clemente routinely kept hopeful batters
   from getting to base.

   _____

6. He was a man of **integrity** who stood by what he believed.

   _____

Name _____

A. Add the prefix to each word. Write the new word on the line.

1. un + known = _____

2. in + credible = _____

3. out + post = _____

4. super + market = _____

5. en + rich = _____

6. un + sightly = _____

---

un- not; opposite	**in-** not; into
en- to make; put into	**super-** above; beyond

B. Read the prefixes and their meanings in the box above. Use the prefixes to help you decode and understand the words below. Circle the prefix in each word. Then write the meaning of each word on the line.

7. independent _____

8. enlarge _____

9. uncommon _____

10. superhuman _____

Name _____

A. Read the draft model. Use the questions that follow the draft to help you think of ways to add a distinctive voice to the text.

Draft Model

The sky was dark. The wind blew hard. A tree crashed in the yard, and the lights went out. My little brother started to cry, but Mom calmly lit candles and started telling us stories.

---

1. How can you change the first sentence to give it an engaging style and tone?

2. What sensory details would help describe the storm?

3. What details would explain the narrator's feelings?

4. What details would show the author's attitude toward the mother?

B. Now revise the draft by adding strong adjectives and verbs to present the information in a more engaging voice.

_____

_____

_____

_____

_____

_____

_____

_____

_____

Name _____

The student who wrote the paragraphs below used text evidence from two different sources to answer the question: *In what ways were the paths to success for Marshall Taylor and Margaret Bourke-White similar?*

Both Marshall Taylor and Margaret Bourke-White met influential people and challenges on their paths to success. As a boy, Marshall met the owners of a bicycle shop who hired him to perform stunts and encouraged him to ride in his first race. Later, he met Louis "Birdie" Munger, a racer who brought him to Massachusetts for training. Margaret Bourke-White was influenced first by her parents, who encouraged her to be whatever she wanted and bought her a camera. Later, she met Henry Luce, a powerful publisher. Luce hired her to work for his magazine, where she became the first female photojournalist.

Both Marshall and Margaret were hard workers who never gave up. These qualities helped them get through the challenges they faced. Even though Marshall had become a professional racer at 18, he couldn't get a hotel room or eat in a restaurant because of discrimination. Margaret also faced challenges. Many businessmen didn't think a woman should photograph places like a steel mill. But Marshall and Margaret prevailed and became role models for many others.

Reread the passage. Follow the directions below.

1. How were Marshall Taylor and Margaret Bourke-White's paths to success similar? **Circle** the thesis statement that introduces the topic.

2. **Draw a box** around a sentence that shows another comparison between Marshall Taylor and Margaret Bourke-White.

3. **Underline** a sentence that shows how formal language is used as the style and tone.

4. **Write** one of the linking verbs on the line.

_____

Name _____

commonplace	initial	invasive	optimal
advocates	designate	insulation	irrational

Finish each sentence using the vocabulary word provided.

1. **(initial)** They had to come up with a new solution when _____

_____ .

2. **(commonplace)** Where I live _____

_____ .

3. **(irrational)** The idea that _____

_____ .

4. **(designate)** I think the plan is _____

_____ .

5. **(optimal)** My mother decided _____

_____ .

6. **(advocates)** We were able to buy new books _____

_____ .

7. **(insulation)** The builders installed _____

_____ .

8. **(invasive)** The vines were pretty to look at, but _____

_____ .

Name _____

Read the selection. Complete the main idea and key details graphic organizer.

Main Idea
Detail
Detail
Detail

Name _____

Read the passage. Use the ask and answer questions strategy to check your understanding of the text.

Trees for a Healthier Africa

12	Environmentalists are calling for people to plant millions of trees in an effort to improve life in Africa. How can planting trees boost the quality of
26	life? Forests in many regions of Africa have not been conserved. Instead of
39	being protected, many trees have been overharvested. Such deforestation
48	can cause dire results. Less rain, more heat, and erosion are just a few of
63	the grim effects of deforestation. These conditions can cause crops to fail,
75	leading to famine. As people compete for resources, conflicts can occur.
86	Environmentalists believe planting and growing large numbers of trees
95	will bring about a positive reversal of deforestation.

Learning to Change 103

106 Knowing the impact of destroying forests may help prevent such ruin

117 in the future. People have learned what went wrong and how to restore

130 the forests. In the past, it was easy to take the trees for granted. Now the

146 people know that when trees cease to exist, the climate, land, and people

159 are all affected. When the trees disappear, they must be replaced.

170 African people have learned about trees and the greenhouse effect.

180 Plants store carbon dioxide (CO_2). When forests rot or burn, they put

192 more CO_2 in the atmosphere, which causes the "greenhouse effect." Gases

203 like CO_2 trap heat close to the earth. The gases work like a glass roof

218 in a greenhouse that holds in the sun's heat. The greenhouse effect can

231 cause our climate to become warmer. People in Africa are learning how

243 to improve their environment by planting and protecting this important

253 resource.

Name _____

RIPPLE Africa—Cook Stoves and Fruit Trees

RIPPLE is a group in Malawi, Africa, that has helped plant millions of fast-growing trees to improve the environment. Some families have received as many as 25 trees. They learn how to cut only the branches for firewood instead of the whole tree. RIPPLE has combined tree planting with a cook stove project. People are taught to build cook stoves with mud bricks. RIPPLE supplies a new fuel for the stoves, which saves trees. They have also helped people grow fruit trees. The trees help with both food and income, which encourage more planting.

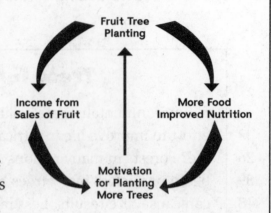

Green Belt Movement—Wangari Maathai

A Nobel Peace Prize winner from Kenya also helped people protect their environment by planting trees. Beginning in 1976, Dr. Wangari Maathai encouraged tree planting. Through a group called The Green Belt Movement, Maathai helped women plant more than 40 million trees. At the United Nations, Dr. Maathai called for all nations to stop taking the trees for granted.

The African Wildlife Foundation

The African Wildlife Foundation (AWF) is another group working hard to reverse deforestation. AWF studied the dwindling forests in an effort to slow CO_2 buildup. They made plans to increase tree growth instead of letting the forests shrink even more. AWF found places where women could grow tree seedlings. The seedlings became a source of income for the women. The AWF bought the trees for replanting after they grew. Dr. Steven Kiruswa is the former AWF Director in Tanzania. He says, "AWF knows the threat of climate change to Africa and is working on ways to reduce CO_2 and deforestation."

What Does It Take?

Reversing deforestation takes time, but many people are working to turn it around. People have chosen not to make the same mistakes again. By working together they hope to improve the earth's environment.

Name _____

A. Reread the passage and answer the questions.

1. What are three details that support the main idea that deforestation can cause dire results?

_____
_____
_____

2. What is the main idea of paragraph 3 on the second page of the passage?

_____
_____

3. What is the main idea of the entire passage?

_____
_____

4. What are two details that support the main idea of this passage?

_____
_____
_____

B. Work with a partner. Read the passage aloud. Pay attention to rate and accuracy. Stop after one minute. Fill out the chart.

	Words Read	–	Number of Errors	=	Words Correct Score
First Read		–		=	
Second Read		–		=	

Name _____

Making Fashion from Plastic Bags

As part of the worldwide movement to "go green," some fashion designers are creating clothing from plastic bags. Here's how: First, flatten three or four bags and use scissors to trim off the handles and bottom seams. Next, layer the bags into one pile. Place paper on top of and below the bags. Next, iron for about fifteen seconds per side. Allow it to cool and then peel away the paper. Use your new plastic fabric to sew dresses, tote bags, wallets, and more.

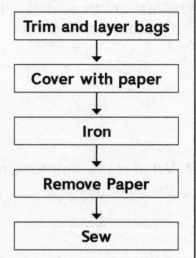

Answer the questions about the text.

1. How do you know this is expository text?

_____

_____

2. What text features does this text include?

_____

3. Is the heading a strong one for this text? Why or why not?

_____

_____

4. What information does the flowchart provide?

_____

_____

Name _____

Read each passage. Look at the word in bold. If the underlined word is a synonym clue write *S* after the passage. If it is an antonym clue, write *A*. Write a definition of the word in bold. Then write a sentence using the word.

1. Forests in many regions of Africa have not been **conserved**. Instead of being protected, many trees have been <u>overharvested</u>. _____

   _____

   _____

2. Such deforestation can cause **dire** results. Less rain, more heat, and erosion are just a few of the <u>grim</u> effects of deforestation. _____

   _____

   _____

3. Knowing the impact of **destroying** forests may help prevent such ruin in the future. People have learned what went wrong and how to <u>restore</u> the forests. _____

   _____

   _____

4. AWF studied the **dwindling** forests in an effort to slow CO_2 buildup. They had the goal of <u>increasing</u> tree growth instead of letting the forests shrink even more. _____

   _____

   _____

5. **Reversing** deforestation takes time, but many people are working to <u>turn it around</u>. _____

   _____

   _____

Name _____

A. Read each sentence. Add either *-ion* **or** *-ation* **to the word in parentheses. Write the new word on the line to complete the sentence.**

1. The **(react)** _____ of the crowd was surprising.

2. In order to use the computers, we will need some **(instruct)**

   _____.

3. The entire school has a high-speed Internet **(connect)**

   _____.

4. Our district has strong **(represent)** _____
   in Congress.

5. What kind of **(consult)** _____ did the counselor
   provide?

6. Painting has always been my favorite form of **(express)**

   _____.

B. Change each verb into a noun by adding *-ion or -ation*. **Each answer will require either dropping or changing the final** *e*.

7. illustrate   _____

8. observe   _____

9. hesitate   _____

10. separate   _____

11. inspire   _____

Name _____

A. Read the draft model. Use the questions that follow the draft to help you think about ways to add opposing claims and counterarguments to help strengthen the writer's argument.

Draft Model

We should all own a reusable shopping bag. This will keep plastic out of our landfills.

---

1. How might readers challenge or criticize the statement in the first sentence? Make this criticism an opposing claim.

2. What would be a good counterargument to that opposing claim?

3. What might be an opposing claim to the statement in the second sentence?

4. What would be a good counterargument to that opposing claim?

B. Now revise the draft by adding opposing claims and counterarguments to those claims.

_____

_____

_____

_____

_____

_____

_____

_____

_____

Name _____

The student who wrote the paragraphs below used text evidence from two different sources to answer the question: *Can recycling, picking up garbage, and promoting mass transit really make a difference in our environment?*

Taking steps to improve the environment—big or small—makes a difference in creating a healthier environment. Big steps like updating a city's mass transit system can result in cleaner air. For example, before the subway system in Athens, Greece, was upgraded, millions of people living there drove cars, which caused pollution. The city built two new metro lines and banned private cars from driving in the commercial district. These changes would "reduce automobile trips to the center of Athens by 250,000 daily." That's a big change!

Even one person can make a big difference. Chad Pregracke started by simply picking up garbage. He eventually founded his own organization and has removed 6 millions pounds of trash from U.S. rivers.

You can make a difference, too. By starting a school recycling program, you can prevent garbage from ending up in rivers in the first place. From one person picking up garbage to a classroom's recycling program to a city's updated subway system, we can all take steps to create a healthier environment.

Reread the passage. Follow the directions below.

1. Can recycling and picking up garbage make a difference? **Circle** the thesis statement that introduces the topic.

2. **Draw a box** around relevant evidence that supports the claim.

3. **Underline** a sentence that summarizes the argument.

4. **Write** one of the irregular verbs on the line.

_____

Name _____

| alignment | calamity | generated | periodic |
| prolonged | tenacity | eclipse | inconvenience |

Use each pair of vocabulary words in a single sentence.

1. calamity, generated

_____

_____

2. prolonged, inconvenience

_____

_____

3. alignment, periodic

_____

_____

4. tenacity, eclipse

_____

_____

Name _____

Read the selection. Complete the author's point of view graphic organizer.

Details	Author's Point of View

Name _____

Read the passage. Use the reread strategy to check details in the text to make sure you understand it.

Preparing for an Inevitable Earthquake

14	If the ground starts to shake, what should you do? The people who need to know are those who live where earthquakes might happen. Having
26	a plan for this kind of crisis can save lives. The state of California has a
41	history of serious earthquakes. People there can reduce the risk of lost
53	lives and property damage. California's Emergency Management Agency
61	tries to prepare everyone.
65	The breaking and shifting of rock plates far below the earth's surface
77	causes earthquakes. Pressure builds between the plates until they finally
87	break free, shifting the earth above. Powerful earthquakes can cause
97	buildings to collapse. Phone service is often lost. Gas and electricity lines
109	can break. Landslides, floods, and fires may take place. In coastal areas,
121	tsunamis can bring huge sea waves over the land. To prepare for these
134	disasters, people must be trained so lives can be saved.

What Rescuers Recommend — 144

147	Surprisingly, one of the greatest dangers is caused by what people do
159	during an earthquake. By instinct, people tend to run outside to escape.
171	Most injuries occur when people try to exit or move within a building.
184	Broken ceilings and windows can injure the person fleeing. Rescue teams
195	from all over the world agree on one thing. To reduce injury and death,
209	people should take three simple steps. The earthquake plan is called
220	"Drop, Cover, and Hold On!" The first step is to *drop down* on your
234	hands and knees. This keeps you from falling if the floor is moving. The
248	next step is to *take cover* under a strong table or desk. *Hold on* to the
264	table tightly. If you don't have a sturdy table, find the closest inside wall.
278	Cover your head and neck with your arms. This sounds easy, but without
291	practicing this procedure often, people may still panic and run.

Name _____

Managing the Risk

Most Californians realize they may someday face an earthquake. The history of California earthquakes goes back more than two hundred years. The first recorded earthquake dates back to 1769 when an explorer felt the ground shaking. In 1906 the San Francisco earthquake lasted less than one minute, yet destroyed the city. Between 225,000 and 300,000 people became homeless. Five major earthquakes have struck since 1906. These major earthquakes have caused California leaders to take action.

The leaders have done research to help reduce loss of life in earthquakes. Lawmakers have made important changes to building codes. Builders must now make homes and buildings better able to withstand an earthquake. They have mapped the land to show which areas would be most affected by an earthquake. Builders are not allowed to build in those high-risk places. Older buildings must have inspections. Dangerous structures must have signs posted so people know the risk. Government programs help fund the repairs.

In countries where buildings are made of mud-brick (adobe), there is much more danger. They are not built to withstand an earthquake. That is when it does make sense to run. In California, most buildings are not as likely to collapse. The stricter building codes have reduced this danger.

G.K. Gilbert/USGS

Preventing Unnecessary Loss

Earthquake scientists, emergency managers, and community leaders are working together in California. People study public school structures to ensure those buildings meet safety codes. The leaders have published a handbook about how to respond to earthquakes. They hold public drills to help people practice the "Drop, Cover, and Hold On!" procedure. A coloring book is available for children with tips on how to stay safe. If everyone prepares for what may come, injuries will be less likely.

Name _____

A. Reread the passage and answer the questions.

1. What fact does the author provide about the cause of most injuries during earthquakes?

   _____

   _____

2. What steps do rescuers recommend that people take to reduce the risk of injury during earthquakes?

   _____

   _____

3. Is the author in favor of these steps? How can you tell?

   _____

   _____

   _____

4. What is the author's point of view about being prepared for earthquakes? Does the author present this point of view objectively? Explain.

   _____

   _____

   _____

B. Work with a partner. Read the passage aloud. Pay attention to rate and accuracy. Stop after one minute. Fill out the chart.

	Words Read	–	Number of Errors	=	Words Correct Score
First Read		–		=	
Second Read		–		=	

Name _____

Reforestation in Guatemala

Entire villages in Guatemala can be wiped out by mudslides. In 2005, Anne Hallum witnessed the horrible effects. She recalled that one couple lost their home and their children in a mudslide. Deforestation, or cutting down trees, is a huge cause of this problem. "We learned the hard way that without trees, we are at risk," said José Avelino Boc, a lemon farmer and Alliance member. Hallum, co-founder of the Alliance for International Reforestation (AIR), has taught Guatemalan villagers to plant trees to protect their forests and villages since 1992. Hallum said, "Food, shade, fertilizer, and mudslide protection—the trees can do it all."

Lloyd Sutton/Alamy

Replanting trees is one way to protect villages from mudslides.

Answer the questions about the text.

1. What text features does this text contain? List two.

   _____

   _____

2. What event does this text first describe? What positive actions happened as a result of the event?

   _____

   _____

3. What do the photograph and caption add to your understanding of mudslides?

   _____

   _____

Name_____

**Read each passage. Underline the paragraph clues that help
you figure out the meaning of each word in bold. Then write the
word's meaning on the line.**

1. In **coastal** areas, tsunamis can bring huge sea waves over the land.
   To prepare for these disasters, people must be trained so lives can
   be saved.

   _____

2. Surprisingly, one of the greatest dangers is caused by what people
   do during an earthquake. By instinct, people tend to run outside to
   escape. Most injuries occur when people try to exit or move within
   a building. Broken ceilings and windows can injure the person
   fleeing.

   _____

3. The earthquake plan is called "Drop, Cover, and Hold On!" The first
   step is to *drop down* on your hands and knees. This keeps you from
   falling if the floor is moving. The next step is to *take cover* under a
   strong table or desk. *Hold on* to the table tightly. If you don't have
   a sturdy table, find the closest inside wall. Cover your head and
   neck with your arms. This sounds easy, but without practicing this
   procedure often, people may still panic and run.

   _____

4. The leaders have done research to help reduce loss of life in
   earthquakes. Lawmakers have made important changes to building
   codes. Builders must now make homes and buildings better able to
   withstand an earthquake.

   _____

Name _____

| permission | inclusion | exclamation |
| division | explosion | explanation |

A. Read each word below. Choose a word from the box that shows the word with the suffix *-ion* added to it. Then write the word on the line.

1. explode   _____

2. permit   _____

3. explain   _____

4. include   _____

5. divide   _____

B. Add the suffix *-ion* to each of the following words. Remember to change the spelling of the word, as needed, to change the word to a noun.

6. admit + ion =   _____

7. collide + ion =   _____

8. omit + ion =   _____

9. transmit + ion =   _____

Name _____

A. Read the draft model. Use the questions that follow the draft to help you think about how to make the order of importance clear to the reader.

Draft Model

There are good reasons to have an earthquake kit. Lights may go out, so you will need flashlights. Gas lines may break, so you will need ready-to-eat food. Water may become undrinkable, so you will need bottled water.

---

1. What is the most important reason to have an earthquake kit? What words or phrases would help show its importance?

2. How can the other reasons be changed or rearranged to help clarify the logical sequence of the text?

3. What sequence words and phrases would help clarify the relationships between the ideas?

B. Now revise the draft by rearranging sentences and adding sequence words and phrases to strengthen the order of importance.

_____

_____

_____

_____

_____

_____

_____

Name _____

The student who wrote the paragraphs below used text evidence from two different sources to answer the question: *Could the Dust Bowl of the 1930s have been prevented?*

If someone like Erica Fernandez would have spoken up in the 1930s, the Dust Bowl could have been prevented. Erica Fernandez prevented a liquefied natural gas facility from being built in her town—along with tons of pollutants it would produce. She did so by educating people about the hazards of such a facility.

For centuries, strong winds have blown across the Great Plains. Natural fires have burned its grasses, but the soil always remained. The grass's strong roots kept the soil in place. The grass grew year after year.

But when farmers planted wheat and corn, these roots died every year. Every year, farmers had to plant new corn and wheat. Then, when extremely strong winds came in the 1930s, the shallow roots couldn't hold the soil.

If someone could have educated farmers about the root issue like Erica educated others about the natural gas facility and its dangers, the farmers might have realized the conditions they were creating. Then they might have decided to use better methods of farming. This might have prevented the Dust Bowl.

Reread the passage. Follow the directions below.

1. Could the Dust Bowl of the 1930s have been prevented? **Circle** the thesis statement that introduces the claim.

2. **Draw a box** around a sequence word that shows the order of events.

3. **Underline** relevant details that support the claim.

4. **Write** one of the pronouns and its antecedent on the line.

_____

Name _____

assess	compensate	deteriorated	devastating
implement	peripheral	potential	summit

Write a complete sentence to answer each question below. In your answer, use the vocabulary word in bold.

1. What new programs would you like your school to **implement**? _____

_____

2. What does your **peripheral** vision help you to see? _____

_____

3. If an athlete goes to practice every day, what does she or he have

the **potential** to do? _____

_____

4. Where is the **summit** of a mountain? _____

_____

5. In a dance contest, what do judges **assess**? _____

_____

6. How can you **compensate** for not doing a homework assignment? _____

_____

7. Why would it be dangerous to walk on a bridge that has

deteriorated? _____

_____

8. What could be **devastating** news to a runner? _____

_____

Name _____

Read the selection. Complete the author's point of view graphic organizer.

Details		Author's Point of View
	→	

Name _____

Read the passage. Use the reread strategy to check for understanding as you read the passage.

Jesse Owens: A Message to the World

	Jesse Owens was an African American track-and-field legend who
11	set world records and won four Olympic gold medals. Without a doubt,
23	Owens had his personal victories at the 1936 Olympic Games held in
35	Berlin, Germany. However, he achieved even more for people worldwide.
45	At that time, Germany was under the reign of the Nazi leader, Adolf Hitler.
59	The Nazis had hoped to prove that white athletes were better than those of
73	all other races. Jesse Owens won four gold medals and dealt a blow to that
88	Nazi myth. Owens was clearly a superior athlete.
96	**Ready, Set, Go!**
99	When Owens was born in 1913, his parents named him James Cleveland
111	Owens. The family moved from Alabama and settled in Ohio in the 1920s
124	in search of a better life. It was there that a teacher mistook his nickname,
139	"J.C.," for "Jesse." His new name stuck. Owens became a track star in high
153	school, setting records in the high jump and running broad jump. He went
166	on to The Ohio State University in 1933, proving to be an outstanding
179	athlete. In 1935, Owens tied world records for the 100-yard dash. He set
192	new world records for the 220-yard dash, the 220-yard low hurdles, and
204	the running broad jump. Owens's success was not just a flash in the pan.
218	He was only warming up for the Olympics.
226	Hitler had made promises not to promote racism during the 1936
237	Olympics. He didn't want to lose the chance to hold the Olympics in
250	Germany. Yet, when the time came, signs of Nazi beliefs were clearly
262	seen in banners, salutes, and symbols. The Nazis wanted to prove that
274	white, blue-eyed people were the best. It was in this tense, unwelcome
286	setting that Jesse Owens competed. Performing to the best of his abilities,
298	Owens proved the Nazis wrong before the whole world—not just once, but
311	four times.

Name _____

Excellence Confronts Discrimination

Owens set new Olympic and world records even though the Nazis called him inferior. Upon returning to America, he needed bold courage again. People cheered his success, but discrimination was a fact of life in America. After all the problems in Germany, Owens still had to ride in the back of the bus at home. He couldn't choose where he wanted to live, because black people did not live in white neighborhoods. Even though he was an American hero, he wasn't invited to the White House for honors.

Despite his problems, Owens was a man who inspired others. He enjoyed speaking at youth groups, sports banquets, and other organizations. Owens loved working with youth. He served as a director and board member for the Chicago Boys' Club. He passed on his life message, "Find the good. It's all around you. Find it, showcase it, and you'll start believing it."

Receiving Recognition

The man who had carried the weight of the world on his shoulders and triumphed at the 1936 Olympics eventually got the honors he deserved. In 1976, Jesse Owens was finally invited to the White House. President Gerald Ford presented him with the Medal of Freedom that year. After Owens's death, President George H. W. Bush awarded him the Congressional Gold Medal in 1990.

Today Owens's desire to help youth continues through the Jesse Owens Foundation. His three daughters work to keep his mission alive. The Foundation provides finances, support, and services to young people to help them go the extra mile and become all they are meant to be.

Jesse Owens won four gold medals at the 1936 Olympics.

Name _____

A. Reread the passage and answer the questions.

1. According to the author, what did Owens achieve at the 1936 Olympic Games?

   _____

   _____

2. According to the author, how did Owens act upon his return to the United States after the Olympics?

   _____

   _____

3. What does the author say about the honors that Owens received from President Ford in 1976 and President Bush in 1990?

   _____

   _____

4. What is the author's point of view about Jesse Owens?

   _____

   _____

B. Work with a partner. Read the passage aloud. Pay attention to intonation. Stop after one minute. Fill out the chart.

	Words Read	–	Number of Errors	=	Words Correct Score
First Read		–		=	
Second Read		–		=	

Name _____

Franklin D. Roosevelt's Battle with Polio

Franklin Delano Roosevelt (FDR) served as the 32nd president of the United States from 1933 to 1945. The only U.S. president elected four times, FDR saw the country through two crises: the Great Depression and World War II. Many Americans at the time were not aware that FDR had suffered a crisis of his own. Diagnosed with polio in 1921, FDR became paralyzed and lived for many years confined to a wheelchair. He did not let his disease slow him down, and he became a champion of polio research. This research finally led to a vaccine in 1955—ten years after FDR's death.

Major Events Related to Franklin D. Roosevelt's Life

Date(s)	Event
1921	Diagnosed with polio
1929–1939	The Great Depression
1933–1945	FDR is president of the United States
1941	United States enters World War II
1945	World War II ends
1945	President Roosevelt dies
1955	Salk Polio vaccine used effectively

Answer the questions about the text.

1. What is your opinion of FDR based on this text?

   _____

   _____

2. How is the information in the table organized? How does it help you understand FDR's years as president?

   _____

   _____

3. Give two examples of additional information that the table presents.

   _____

   _____

Name _____

A. Read each passage. Figure out the meaning of the idiom in bold by looking at the context and the literal meaning of the words. Write the meaning of the idiom on the line.

1. Owens tied world records for the 100-yard dash. He set new world records for the 220-yard dash, the 220-yard low hurdles, and the running broad jump. Owens's success was not just a **flash in the pan.** He was only warming up for the Olympics.

   _____

2. The man who had **carried the weight of the world** on his shoulders and triumphed at the 1936 Olympics eventually got the honors he deserved.

   _____

3. The Foundation provides finances, support, and services to young people to help them **go the extra mile** and become all they are meant to be.

   _____

B. Use each idiom below in a sentence of your own.

1. flash in the pan: _____

   _____

2. carried the weight of the world on his/her shoulders: _____

   _____

3. go the extra mile: _____

   _____

Name _____

resident	metallic	national
competition	criminal	invitation

A. For each word below, find the related word in the box and write it on the line. Circle the vowel or vowel team that sounds different from the original word.

1. nation _____

2. compete _____

3. reside _____

4. invite _____

5. crime _____

6. metal _____

B. Match each word in the left column with its related word in the right column. Circle the vowel that changes its vowel sound.

7. acquire natural

8. nature decision

9. decide collision

10. ignite acquisition

11. collide ignition

Name _____

A. Read the draft model. Use the questions that follow the draft to help you think about what transitions you can add to connect ideas and indicate time order.

Draft Model

My brother was born healthy. He developed a heart problem. His weak heart made him sick.

---

1. When was the brother born in the list of events? What transition word or phrase could help the reader understand the order?

2. When did he develop his heart problem? What transitions could help the reader understand the order?

3. What transitions would help the reader understand why the brother's heart problem led to sickness?

B. Now revise the draft by adding transitions to connect ideas and to show when events took place.

_____

_____

_____

_____

_____

_____

_____

Name _____

The student who wrote the paragraphs below used text evidence from two different sources to answer the question: *Is it necessary to exercise regularly?*

Exercising regularly is absolutely necessary. Many people sit all day at school or work. That isn't good for their physical health. They need to exercise to get moving! Our brains need oxygen to stay alert. Breathing deeply during aerobic exercise moves oxygen to all parts of the body, including to the brain. Aerobic exercises like walking, swimming, or mountain climbing also help bring oxygen to cells. Cells need oxygen so they can turn food into energy.

Exercise is not only good for a person's physical health, it is good for a person's mental health, too. Erik Weilhenmayer was blind by the time he was thirteen. As his sight gradually failed, Erik still exercised by playing sports and riding his bike. When he turned 14, his mother died. To help him cope with his blindness and the loss of his mother, Erik's father took him and his siblings on trips around the world, including rock-climbing trips. These trips inspired Erik to begin rock climbing, scuba diving, and sky-diving. Through exercise, Erik continues to cope with and conquer challenges.

Exercising regularly keeps people healthy—both physically and mentally.

Reread the passage. Follow the directions below.

1. Why is exercise necessary? **Circle** text evidence that supports the claim.

2. **Draw a box** around a transitional sentence that moves the reader from one idea to the next.

3. **Underline** the conclusion that summarizes the claim.

4. **Write** a subject pronoun and an object pronoun on the line.

_____

Name _____

benefactor	empathy	endeavor	entail
extensive	indecision	multitude	tentatively

Finish each sentence using the vocabulary word provided.

1. **(multitude)** In the springtime, the park _____

   _____

2. **(tentatively)** I wasn't sure if I liked the music, _____

   _____

3. **(entail)** Does being on the dance team _____

   _____

4. **(extensive)** Doing well on the test requires _____

   _____

5. **(indecision)** After an hour of _____

   _____

6. **(benefactor)** Our school needed money to buy books for the library, _____

   _____

7. **(empathy)** I was new at the school last year, _____

   _____

8. **(endeavor)** My bedroom is an absolute mess, _____

   _____

Name _____

Read the selection. Complete the theme graphic organizer.

Detail

↓

Detail

↓

Detail

↓

Theme

Name _____

Read the passage. Use the summarize strategy to check your understanding.

Decisions

11	**Scene 1:** *Shama's bedroom in the afternoon. The walls are plastered with posters depicting Shama's favorite band, The Black Hats. Shama is*
22	*sitting at her desk, frantically typing on her computer while she talks on her*
36	*telephone.*
37	**Shama** *(worried)*: I can't get on the ticket site. Something's not
48	functioning properly. It's just NOT right. What? Are you certain? *(growing*
59	*more upset)* The concert is sold out? Is there anything I can do? *(brief*
73	*pause)* Good-bye. *(Hangs up the phone and lets out a wail. The door*
86	*opens, and Shama's older brother, Danny, walks into her room.)*
96	**Danny:** Are you okay?
100	**Shama:** Not okay—a total wreck, actually. The concert is sold out. *(She*
113	*abruptly begins to bawl.)* I desperately wanted to go.
122	**Danny:** Yeah, your anticipation level was up there. I'm sorry.
132	**Shama** *(sniffling and wiping away her tears)*: Oh, well, Ms. Allie
143	wanted to know if I could babysit the twins that night because it's her
157	wedding anniversary. I suppose now I can tell her "yes."
167	**Danny:** Better you than me. Those twins are an absolute nightmare. I
179	babysat them once and vowed never to do it again.
189	**Scene 2:** *It's a few weeks later, and Shama is on her bed, reading a book.*
205	*We hear her mother calling.*
210	**Mother's Voice:** Shama? *(Sound of footsteps pounding up the stairs.)*
220	That racket you hear is Rhonda running up the stairs.
230	**Rhonda** *(excitedly)*: I have unbelievably awesome news! Someone gave
239	my aunt tickets to the concert tonight, and she has no desire to go, so
254	guess which lucky duo gets them?
260	**Shama** *(jumping up in excitement)*: Yes! *(grimacing and letting out a*
271	*groan)* Oh no! I told my neighbor I would babysit.

Name _____

Rhonda: Just cancel. This is definitely more important.

Shama: It's her anniversary, so I can't just leave her in the lurch.

Rhonda: That's total insanity. It's the Black Hats, your all-time favorite band, and who knows when they'll return? On the other hand, wedding anniversaries come every single solitary year!

Shama: You're right. Maybe she won't object to celebrating tomorrow, instead, since it's not like they won't still be married.

Scene 3: *Shama is standing in front of Ms. Allie's door. Just as she starts to knock, Ms. Allie pulls into the driveway and then gets out of the car with shopping bags.*

Ms. Allie: Hi, Shama! I just bought the most extraordinary dress for my anniversary dinner, and we got a reservation at the hottest new restaurant. I can't tell you how ecstatic I am that you agreed to babysit for us. It will be the perfect tenth anniversary!

Shama *(trying to look happy)*: Great. I just wanted to confirm. See you tonight.

Scene 4: *Shama's kitchen. Danny is hunched over his homework at the cluttered kitchen table. Shama enters.*

Shama: Hi, magnificent brother. Rhonda got me a ticket for the Black Hats tonight, but I've committed to babysitting the twins—

Danny: I know what you're going to ask, and no, I absolutely can't accommodate you on this one. Not only are those twins a nightmare, but also I have homework. Plus, I promised Mom I would finally clean my room.

Shama: What if I promise to clean your disgusting, germ-filled room? I assure you it will be immaculate.

Danny: Not worth it.

Shama: What if I promise to clean your room for a month?

Danny: A month? That sounds pretty equivalent to a night with the terrible twins. It's a deal.

Shama: Yes! Black Hats, here I come.

Name _____

A. Reread the passage and answer the questions.

1. In Scene 2 of the play, what conflict does Shama have?

   _____

   _____

2. In Scene 3, why does Shama go to Ms. Allie's house? What happens?

   _____

   _____

   _____

   _____

3. In Scene 4, how does Danny react when Shama first asks him to babysit in her place so she can go to the concert? What does Shama promise to do to get him to agree?

   _____

   _____

   _____

4. What do you think is the theme, or message, of this play?

   _____

   _____

B. Work with a partner. Read the passage aloud. Pay attention to expression. Stop after one minute. Fill out the chart.

	Words Read	–	Number of Errors	=	Words Correct Score
First Read		–		=	
Second Read		–		=	

Name _____

Hard Rock!

SCENE 2 *The basement of Scott's house; Scott tunes his guitar and Jake adjusts his drum set.*

SCOTT *(strumming the guitar)*: Hey, Jake. Are you ready to hear the new song I wrote?

JAKE: Sure, why not? Let's hear it.

Scott turns his amplifier up and begins to strum loudly and sing in a raspy voice. As the song increases in volume and intensity, Jake gets up and paces around the room uncomfortably. He taps his foot nervously as Scott finishes the song with three loud chords—bomp, bomp, BOHHHHMP—and a fierce scream into the microphone.

SCOTT *(breaking the sudden silence)*: So . . . what do you think? It'll be our first big hit, right?

JAKE *(stroking his chin, as if deep in thought)*: Um, well, it is original. I mean, I've never heard anything quite like it before . . . *(His voice trails off.)*

SCOTT: Awesome! I knew you'd like it.

Answer the questions about the text.

1. List three text features that let you know this text is drama.

   _____

2. Which text feature tells you where the action takes place?

   _____

3. Where in the play do you think this scene takes place? Explain.

   _____

   _____

4. What do you think Jake's conflict is? Does he resolve it?

   _____

   _____

Name _____

A. Write the definition for each word below. Then provide a homophone for each word.

1. bawl _____

2. wail _____

3. night _____

4. stairs _____

5. groan _____

B. Finish each sentence two ways, once for each of the homophones provided.

6. (right/write) I will _____

   I will _____

7. (sight/site) The new school will _____

   The new school will _____

8. (your/you're) I love to dance _____

   I love to dance _____

9. (great/grate) Last night, my mom _____

   Last night, my mom _____

Name _____

A. Read each sentence. Circle the word that has a prefix. Then write the meaning of the word on the line.

1. The players thought it was unfair that the same pitcher ended each game.

   _____

2. The jeweler was able to reattach the band to the watch.

   _____

3. Does this clue enable you to solve the mystery?

   _____

4. With her amazing speed, she could easily outdistance the other runners.

   _____

unhappiness	discouragement	unselfishly
enjoyment	retirement	distrustful

B. Write the prefix and the suffix for each word. Then write the word in the box above that has the same prefix and the same suffix.

	Prefix	Suffix	Word with the Same Prefix and Same Suffix
5. disappointment	_____	_____	_____
6. unpleasantness	_____	_____	_____
7. disgraceful	_____	_____	_____
8. enforcement	_____	_____	_____

Name _____

A. Read the draft model. Use the questions that follow the draft to help you think about how adding dialogue would help develop the characters.

Draft Model

"Let's do something to help Lucy with her math," Hiram suggested. Jarel asked, "What should we do?"

---

1. What additional dialogue would tell readers more about Hiram's personality?

2. What dialogue would tell readers more about Jarel?

3. What other words could Jarel and Hiram say to show how each one feels about Lucy?

4. What language would convey the characters' tone of voice?

B. Now revise the draft by adding dialogue and other details to help develop the characters.

_____

_____

_____

_____

_____

_____

_____

_____

Name _____

The student who wrote the scene below used details from two different sources to answer the prompt: *Write a flashback scene between Bucho and Joe in which Bucho makes a difficult decision.*

JOE: This English test is stupid.

[*Bucho doesn't hear Joe. He is concentrating on his own test.*]

JOE: Hey, Bucho.

BUCHO: Huh?

JOE: This stupid English test is killing me.

BUCHO: Hmmm.

JOE: Move your arm—let me see your paper.

BUCHO: Uh ... I don't think so, Joe.

JOE: What? But we're friends! You used to let me cheat all the time.

BUCHO: Whatever. Not anymore, ok?

JOE: IF you don't let me see your test, you can forget about being friends.

BUCHO: Sorry, dude.

[*Bucho gets up to hand his test in.*]

Reread the passage. Follow the directions below.

1. How is Bucho's character changing? **Circle** text evidence that shows how Bucho is becoming more responsible.

2. **Draw a box** around dialogue that helps you make inferences about Joe's intelligence.

3. What decision did Bucho have to make? **Underline** the sentence that shows Bucho's point of view about cheating.

4. **Write** one of the possessive pronouns on the line.

_____

Name _____

| adjustment | chattering | ember | mentor |
| nomadic | sturdy | rapport | reunites |

Write a complete sentence to answer each question below.
In your answer, use the vocabulary word in bold.

1. Why might people **chattering** in a movie theater bother you?

   _____

2. Why would it be dangerous to pick up an **ember** with your
   bare hands?

   _____

3. Why might going to a new school be a difficult **adjustment**?

   _____

   _____

4. Why might it be useful to have a **mentor**?

   _____

5. How would you describe **nomadic** people?

   _____

6. Why shouldn't you sit in a chair that is not **sturdy**?

   _____

7. What is an occasion that often **reunites** family members?

   _____

8. Why is it important to have a **rapport** with the people you are
   friends with?

   _____

Name _____

Read the selection. Complete the theme graphic organizer.

```
┌─────────────────────────────────────────────┐
│ Detail                                      │
│                                             │
│                                             │
│                                             │
└─────────────────────────────────────────────┘
                      │
                      ▼
┌─────────────────────────────────────────────┐
│ Detail                                      │
│                                             │
│                                             │
│                                             │
└─────────────────────────────────────────────┘
                      │
                      ▼
┌─────────────────────────────────────────────┐
│ Detail                                      │
│                                             │
│                                             │
│                                             │
└─────────────────────────────────────────────┘
                      │
                      ▼
┌─────────────────────────────────────────────┐
│ Theme                                       │
│                                             │
│                                             │
│                                             │
└─────────────────────────────────────────────┘
```

Read the passage. Use the summarize strategy to check your understanding.

DELAYED

	DELAYED, DELAYED, DELAYED read the Departure Board.
7	**All flights in and out of Chicago were stalled**
16	**by the howling winds outside.**
21	Rosie stared hard at **Delight Flight 2040 Chicago to Boston.**
31	—*Change, Change, Change!* she yelled silently at the board.
40	*Get me out of Chicago!*
45	Suddenly the Departure Board flickered and Rosie held her breath.
55	DELAYED blinked and changed . . . to CANCELLED.
61	—*STUCK, JUST MY LUCK!*
65	Next to her, another girl gave a gasp.
73	—*¡¿CANCELADO!? ¿Por qué?*
76	Rosie saw tears in her eyes.
82	*She must be scared.*
86	—*What's your name?* Rosie asked.
91	—*Me llamo Estrella,* said the girl.
97	Pointing to the board, she said,
103	—*Y mi vuelo se cancela.*
108	—*Look, and you'll see why,* said Rosie.
115	A blizzard was swirling outside the large windows.
123	Estrella's mouth dropped open and she rushed over to look.
133	—*This is . . .?* said Estrella, her eyes wide.
140	—*Snow, said Rosie. —You have never seen snow?*
148	—*No snow in Panama,* Estrella explained.

Name _____

—I've seen plenty of snow, up to here.
    I've had it with snow, Rosie said.
    And I want to get home!

—Yo quiero ir a casa, said Estrella.
She wants to go home, too.
And home is so far away.

Just then the airport speakers
gave a loud crackle.
—Attention ALL passengers! ALL flights are cancelled.

Poor Estrella looks so scared.
—Me llamo Rosie. Let me help you,
Rosie said to the girl.

Rosie spoke to a person at the counter.
—I need to get to Boston,
    and my friend needs to get to Panama.

While they waited, Rosie took
    Estrella's arm.
—Come, said Rosie to Estrella.
    Let's go look at the snow!

They wheeled their bags to the
    window.
Being stuck together might be better
than being stuck alone.

Name _____

A. Reread the passage and answer the questions.

1. At the beginning of the passage, how is Rosie feeling? Why?

_____

_____

2. How does Estrella's situation compare with Rosie's?

_____

_____

3. In the last four stanzas, what does Rosie do? What does she think
   in the last stanza?

_____

_____

_____

4. How do Rosie's feelings change by the end of the passage? Based
   on these details, what do you think is the theme of this passage?

_____

_____

**B. Work with a partner. Read the passage aloud. Pay attention to
intonation. Stop after one minute. Fill out the chart.**

	Words Read	–	Number of Errors	=	Words Correct Score
First Read		–		=	
Second Read		–		=	

Name _____

Worlds Apart

I hope the seat next to me stays empty!
I'd love to get some reading done in flight.
I'll just sit down, spread out my things,
And open my novel, *Worlds Apart.*

There's a tall man standing over me, smiling.
Perdone, señorita. Este es mi asiento.
What in the world did he just say? I don't know what to do!
Perdone, señorita.

I'd better move my things to give the man room.
So much for that empty seat! *Gracias,* he says.
He's reaching into his briefcase.
Pulling out his own book *Mundos Aparte.*

Oh, I can't believe this! Of all books!
Excuse me, sir! He won't believe this.
Ah, sí. Worlds Apart. *Buen libro!*
Laughter between two strangers fills the plane.

Answer the questions about the text.

1. What elements of free-verse fiction can you find in this text?

_____

_____

2. Based on this interior monologue, how would you describe the main character?

_____

3. What does the last stanza tell you about the characters?

_____

_____

Name_____

A. Homographs are words that are spelled the same but have different meanings. Write a new sentence using a homograph of each word in bold.

1. All flights in and out of Chicago were stalled by the howling **winds** outside.

_____

2. *Change, Change, Change!* she yelled silently at the board.

_____

3. **Just** then the airport speakers gave a loud crackle.

_____

4. Rosie **spoke** to a person at the counter.

_____

B. Write a definition for both homographs in each sentence below. Write the definitions in the order the words appear in the sentence.

5. I **spoke** to Hector about the broken **spoke** on his bike.

_____

6. As the fierce **winds** blow, the car **winds** along the mountain road.

_____

7. After I **change** this dollar, I will have **change** for the vending machine.

_____

8. The speaker **just** said, "No one would be hungry in a **just** world."

_____

Name _____

proportion	copilot	transformation	postpone
submit	combine	transparent	cooperate
profession	companion	suburb	postwar

A. Sort each word in the box based on its prefix. Write each word in the correct column.

co-	com-	post-
_____	_____	_____
_____	_____	_____

pro-	sub-	trans-
_____	_____	_____
_____	_____	_____

B. Read each sentence. Circle the word that has a prefix. Then write the meaning of the prefix on the line.

1. The submarine slipped beneath the waves. _____

2. I decided to transfer to a more challenging dance class.

   _____

3. The postgame celebration starts at 5:30. _____

4. People on the commission voted on the plans for a new park.

   _____

5. The co-workers at the restaurant agreed to switch their shifts.

   _____

Name

A. Read the draft model. Use the questions that follow the draft to help you add details and events to develop the plot.

Draft Model

Jojo watched as the movers carried the boxes into the house. She wished she were still in her old home in her old neighborhood. A boy Jojo's age came out from next door.

---

1. What events and details could be added to tell readers more about Jojo?

2. What events or details could be added to help make the conflict clearer?

3. What details would show how Jojo is affected by meeting a new neighbor?

B. Now revise the draft by adding details and events to help develop the plot. Your details and events should show readers more about what happens between Jojo and the neighbor and how the events affect Jojo.

_____

_____

_____

_____

_____

_____

_____

The student who wrote the paragraphs below used text evidence from two different sources to respond to the prompt: *Imagine that Aminata and Kek were both in Ms. Hernandez's ESL class. Write a diary entry from Mrs. Hernandez's point of view describing her impressions of Aminata and Kek on their first day.*

Today, two new students came to my ESL class: Aminata and Kek. I am so proud of both of them! I remember how scary it was to come here and not know a word of English. I used to sit at my tiny desk and look at picture books to try to find out what the stories said. Kek may have been nervous, but he was eager to get started right away. His enthusiasm made me laugh! I hope he didn't think I was laughing at him. I don't think he did, because he laughed, too.

Aminata seemed shy and nervous at first, but when she finally gave her presentation, I had goose bumps. She was able to communicate with everyone in the room. When she "told" us about reuniting with her father, tears came to my eyes. It reminds me that we are all the same—humans with hearts. And we are all connected to each other, even though we don't look the same or speak the same language.

Reread the passage. Follow the directions below.

1. When did Ms. Hernandez move to the United States? **Circle** a sentence that helps readers infer this information.

2. **Draw a box** around a sentence that shows Ms. Hernendez's point of view.

3. **Underline** a strong conclusion that Ms. Hernandez makes in her diary entry.

4. **Write** one example of pronoun/verb agreement on the line.

_____

Name _____

| lounge | obligation | answerable | proportion |

Finish each sentence using the vocabulary word provided.

1. **(obligation)** If you make a promise to a good friend, _____

_____.

2. **(lounge)** At my school, the teachers _____

_____.

3. **(proportion)** The artist did an excellent job _____

_____.

4. **(answerable)** The students at the school _____

_____.

Name _____

Read the selection. Complete the point of view graphic organizer.

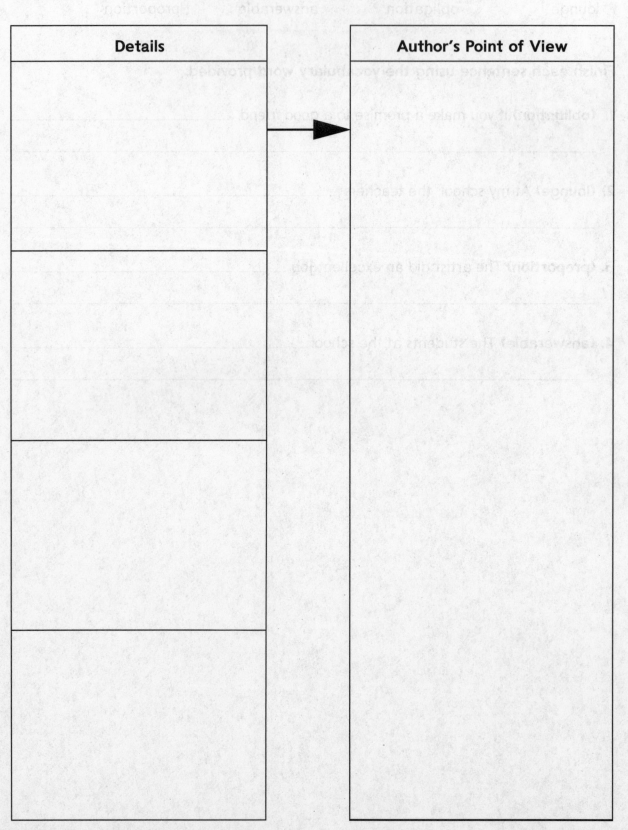

Details	Author's Point of View

Name_____

Read the poem. Check your understanding by asking yourself what point of view the poem is told from.

Dear Lola,

2	It's been a full day since you've gone missing and
12	I've been a bundle of nerves.
18	Time and again I strain to hear you scratching,
27	scratching at the door. Or see your face as you
37	come barreling down the street.
42	I've put up posters and pounded the pavement
50	for hours, wishing I had gotten that back gate
59	fixed faster. Then you would still be here, softly
68	snoring in your battered, blue bed, instead of
76	outside scared and alone. I miss you, Lola.
84	I'm wishing on a star that I find you SOON!
94	Love, Carolyn

Dear Carolyn,

96	
98	You won't believe the adventure
103	I've been having! It's been a wild ride!
111	The gate was open, so I raced right out
120	and chased a squirrel for miles. After that,
128	I was lost. I was scared stiff at first,
137	but then a nice woman took me in. She
146	gave me food and made a big bed for me.
156	This morning we walked past a poster
163	with a picture that looks a lot like me.
172	She smiled and said that big changes will
180	be just around the corner. She says I'll
188	have a visitor soon. I hope it's you.
196	Love, Lola

Image Source/PunchStock

Name _____

A. Reread the passage and answer the questions.

1. Who is the speaker in the first letter of the poem? What does the first letter tell you about the speaker?

_____

_____

2. Who is the speaker in the second letter of the poem? What does the second letter tell you about this speaker?

_____

_____

3. What point of view is each letter written from? How do you know?

_____

_____

_____

4. What do you learn about the story because of this point of view?

_____

_____

_____

B. Work with a partner. Read the passage aloud. Pay attention to expression and phrasing. Stop after one minute. Fill out the chart.

	Words Read	–	Number of Errors	=	Words Correct Score
First Read		–		=	
Second Read		–		=	

Name _____

Cheering Up Callie

Callie was sullen, sad
Since her friend Frances had moved far away.
Her brother Ben wanted to cheer her up,
But nothing he said seemed suitably soothing.
Callie just sat in a chair, staring out the window.
Then Ben had an idea;
He started making funny faces and silly sounds,
Flipping backward like a jumping monkey.
He cracked her up with his antics,
And at last, she burst into giggles.

Answer the questions about the text.

1. How do you know that "Cheering Up Callie" is free verse?

_____

_____

_____

2. How do you know this text is narrative poetry?

_____

_____

_____

3. Write two examples of alliteration used in the poem. Circle the letter or letters of each repeated sound.

_____

_____

Name _____

> **Alliteration** is the repetition of a consonant sound at the beginnings of words near one another.
>
> **Assonance** is the repetition of a vowel sound inside words near one another.
>
> Poets use both devices to add a musical quality to a poem and to draw attention to certain words, phrases, or ideas.

Read the lines of the free verse poem below. Then answer the questions.

You won't believe the adventure
I've been having! It's been a wild ride!
The gate was open, so I raced right out
and chased a squirrel for miles. After that,
I was lost. I was scared stiff at first,
but then a nice woman took me in. She gave
me food and made a big bed for me. This
morning we walked past a poster with a picture
that looks a lot like me.

1. Find two examples of alliteration in the lines above. Write them below.

   _____

2. Find one example of assonance. Write it below.

   _____

3. Read the passage aloud. How do alliteration and assonance add to your enjoyment of reading the passage?

   _____

   _____

4. Write a short poem about an animal walking or running. Use at least one example of alliteration and one example of assonance.

   _____

   _____

Name _____

Read each passage. Use context clues to help you figure out the meaning of each idiom in bold. Then write the idiom's meaning on the line.

1. It's been a full day since you've gone missing and I've been **a bundle of nerves**.

   _____

2. Or see your face as you come **barreling** down the street.

   _____

3. I've put up posters and **pounded the pavement** for hours, wishing I had gotten that back gate fixed faster.

   _____

4. You won't believe the adventure I've been having! It's been **a wild ride**!

   _____

5. I was **scared stiff** at first, but then a nice woman took me in.

   _____

6. She smiled and said that big changes will be **just around the corner**.

   _____

Name _____

| magic | office | public | reject | design |

A. Read each sentence. Underline the word that has a suffix that causes consonant alternation. Then choose the related base word from the box above and write the word on the line.

1. My brother was disappointed when he got the rejection letter. _____

2. The restaurant got publicity by donating food to the event. _____

3. I was surprised the magician had tricks that were so clever! _____

4. We decided to designate my sister as our team leader. _____

5. The mayor had an official ceremony her first day on the job. _____

B. Circle the word that matches each clue below.

6. The *b* is silent in the base word, but not in the word with the suffix added.

   birthday   crumble   babbling

7. The *c* in the base word sounds like a *k* when the suffix is added.

   official   prejudicial   muscular

8. The suffix creates the *sh* sound, but the base word has the *s* sound.

   prejudicial   justice   prejudge

9. The *n* is now heard, but the sound is not in the original base word.

   solemn   solemnity   sanity

Name _____

A. Read the draft model. Use the questions that follow the draft to help you add sensory language to create a more vivid picture in the reader's mind.

Draft Model

The spade digs in the ground.
It lifts the crumbling clods of dirt.

Then it gently covers the tiny seeds.
The soil smells like spring.

---

1. What do the crumbling clods of dirt look like? Is there anything in the dirt?

2. In the third line, what is "it"?

3. When were the seeds planted? What do the seeds look like in the dirt?

4. In the last line, exactly how does the soil smell like spring?

B. Now revise the draft by adding sensory language. Your changes should help bring to life the speaker's experience.

_____

_____

_____

_____

_____

_____

The student who wrote the poem below used examples from two different sources to respond to the prompt: *Write a free-verse poem about a time when you've taken responsibility for your actions.*

Beep! Beep!
said my clock.
"Do I have to?"
I asked myself.
"I don't think so,"
I fluffed my pillow.
"It's a cold, stay-in day."
So I didn't take the garbage out.
And soon, I had to pay.
Because my dog took the garbage,
but he didn't take it out.
He ripped it, spilled it, and spread it
throughout the whole stinking house.
From underneath my cozy blankets
it hit me like a truck.
A putrid-waft alarm clock that signaled
Time to clean it all up.

Reread the passage. Follow the directions below.

1. What finally got the narrator out of bed? **Circle** the sensory language that reveals how the narrator got out of bed.

2. **Draw a box** around a sentence that shows the narrator's point of view.

3. How does the narrator take responsibility for his actions? **Underline** a strong conclusion of the poem.

4. **Write** one relative pronoun and what it refers to on the line.

Name _____

audacity	deception	desolate	exploits
oblivious	somber	steadfast	valiant

Use each pair of vocabulary words in a single sentence.

1. audacity, deception

_____

_____

2. desolate, somber

_____

_____

3. valiant, steadfast

_____

_____

4. oblivious, exploits

_____

_____

Name _____

**Read the selection. Complete the problem and solution
graphic organizer.**

Character

Setting

Problem

Events

↓

↓

Solution

Name _____

**Read the passage. Use the make, confirm, and revise
predictions strategy to check your understanding as you read.**

Athena and Arachne

12	Long ago when Greek gods and goddesses roamed the Earth, there lived a young maiden by the name of Arachne who was known far and wide for
27	her skillful weaving. She could pull beautiful threads from fluffy wool and
39	twirl a spindle until it appeared to be dancing. The cloths she wove had
53	such magnificent patterns and images that women came from all over to
65	gaze upon them with wonder.
70	Those who saw her work said that surely she had been tutored by
83	Athena, the goddess of weaving. When Arachne heard this, she scoffed and
95	said she had taught herself. She even went so far as to claim that her skills
111	were superior to those of Athena, disrespectfully mocking the goddess by
122	declaring, "Let the goddess try to match her skills against mine."
133	Now, it is a foolish thing to both mock and challenge the gods,
146	especially the Greek gods, but that did not stop Arachne, who was as
159	vain as she was talented. "I have confidence I will best her, and if not,
174	I will accept the penalty of losing."
181	Athena was greatly displeased when she heard of Arachne's claims,
191	and she decided to pay the maiden a visit. To give Arachne a chance to
206	apologize for her boasting, Athena disguised herself as an old lady. She
218	wore her hair gray and thinning, lined her face with the wisdom of years,
232	and used a stick to walk.
238	Athena approached Arachne and spoke to her. "Your skill as a weaver
250	is renowned, and I can see that you do your craft well. However, it would
265	serve you to be more humble and not set yourself above the gods and
279	goddesses. You should yield the goddess Athena's place to her and take
291	back your boastful words. I'm sure Athena would pardon you if you made
304	amends to her."

Name _____

Arachne stared at the old woman and said disdainfully, "I don't need anyone's advice but my own. Athena is welcome to come here and try and match my skills, unless of course she is afraid of losing."

At those bold and foolish words, the old woman cast off her disguise and said, "It is I, Athena, and since it is a contest you want, it is a contest you shall get."

Arachne blushed when she realized to whom she was speaking, but she did not change her resolve. The contest began at once.

The goddess and mortal took their places at looms. They wove thread in and out at a furious pace, and it didn't take long for images to begin appearing on the cloth, such was the skill of the weavers.

Athena's images portrayed the power of the gods against various mortals who had displeased them. Her images were meant as a warning to Arachne that her pride was both unwise and dangerous.

Arachne ignored the warning, and the images she wove were scenes of the gods and goddesses doing foolish things. The gods were shown as feeble and reckless. Arachne's work was flawless and beautiful but full of scorn for the gods and goddesses.

Incensed at Arachne's disrespect, Athena ripped up Arachne's cloth. Arachne cried out at seeing her work destroyed. In response, Athena said to her, "You are foolish and vain, but I can see you love your craft, so I will take pity on you and not kill you. Instead, I will let you spin forever." With those words, she sprinkled a magic juice upon Arachne. Arachne's body shrank, her limbs changed, and her fingers turned into legs. Her belly grew round, and from it came a fine thread. Athena had turned Arachne into a spider to pursue her skill as a weaver by making and remaking spider webs.

Name _____

A. Reread the passage and answer the questions.

1. How does Arachne create a problem for herself?

   _____

   _____

2. How does Arachne try to prove that her weaving is better
   than Athena's?

   _____

   _____

3. Even though Athena is displeased with Arachne, she wants to give
   Arachne a chance to apologize. Does this solution work? Explain.

   _____

   _____

4. At the end of the story, Athena's problem is that she wants to
   punish Arachne for making fun of the gods. Yet she appreciates
   Arachne's love of weaving. How does Athena solve this problem?

   _____

   _____

**B. Work with a partner. Read the passage aloud. Pay attention to
intonation and phrasing. Stop after one minute. Fill out the chart.**

	Words Read	–	Number of Errors	=	Words Correct Score
First Read		–		=	
Second Read		–		=	

Name _____

The Wings of Icarus

"What are you making, Dad?" Icarus asked his father, Daedalus. He was constructing something from wax and feathers. The two had been imprisoned in the labyrinth his father had created for King Minos—an irony that was getting the best of Daedalus's temper.

"You'll see, Icarus. We will show that crazy king who's smarter," Daedalus declared. "Here, Son, try these on." Daedulus handed him a pair of wings made from wax and feathers.

"You're kidding, right, Dad?" Icarus replied.

"Not at all. Use these wings to escape," Daedalus ordered, fastening the wings to his son's body. "Now go, but don't fly too close to the sun."

As he soared, Icarus felt invigorated and powerful. Forgetting his father's warning, he flew higher—almost touching the sun. Suddenly, Icarus felt his wings getting heavy, and before he knew it, he dropped to the sea below. Sadly, Icarus drowned. The Icarian Sea was named in his honor.

Answer the questions about the text.

1. What element found in most myths does the text contain?

   _____

   _____

2. In your opinion, what lesson does this text teach?

   _____

   _____

3. Describe the series of events that contribute to the text's larger-than-life quality.

   _____

   _____

   _____

Name _____

In your own words, write a definition of the word in bold in each sentence below. Use the context of the sentence and the information about the word's origin to help you.

1. The cloths she wove had such **magnificent** patterns and images that women came from all over to gaze upon them with wonder.

   Origin: Latin *magnificus* meaning "noble in character"

   Definition: _____

2. She even went so far as to claim that her skills were **superior** to those of Athena, disrespectfully mocking the goddess by declaring, "Let the goddess try to match her skills against mine."

   Origin: Latin *superiorem* meaning "higher"

   Definition: _____

3. At those bold and foolish words, the old woman cast off her **disguise** and said, "It is I, Athena, and since it is a contest you want, it is a contest you shall get."

   Origin: Ancient French, *deguiser,* meaning "a change from the usual dress or appearance"

   Definition: _____

4. Athena's images **portrayed** the power of the gods against various mortals who had displeased them.

   Origin: Latin, *protrahere,* meaning "to reveal"

   Definition: _____

Name_____

miner	naval	vane	pane	sheer
navel	pain	shear	minor	vein

A. Find the homophone pairs in the box. Write each pair on a line.

1. _____

2. _____

3. _____

4. _____

5. _____

B. Draw a line from each word in the left column to its homophone in the right column. Then choose one homophone pair and use both words in a sentence.

6. principle   vain

7. aisle   idle

8. lesson   principal

9. idol   isle

10. vein   lessen

11. _____

_____

_____

Name _____

A. Read the draft model. Use the questions that follow the draft to help you think about what transitions you can add to indicate shifts in time or setting and to connect plot events.

Draft Model

Jacob heard Dragon was threatening the kingdom. He decided to visit Dragon. He left for the journey to Dragon's cave. Jacob arrived at the cave.

---

1. What transitional words and phrases would help show readers when it was that Jacob heard about Dragon threatening the kingdom? What transitions would show when Jacob decided to visit Dragon?

2. What transitions would help show the connections between the events in the first and second sentences?

3. What transitions would help indicate shifts in setting?

B. Now revise the draft by adding transitions to help clarify shifts in time and setting and to help connect plot events.

_____

_____

_____

_____

_____

_____

_____

_____

Name _____

The student who wrote the paragraphs below used details from two different sources to respond to the prompt: *Rewrite the story of Icarus's escape as a parody, as if it were included in "The A-MAZE-ing Tale of Theseus and the Minotaur."*

When Icarus saw Adriadne running toward the boat, he moaned. She was leaving without him—and with Theseus. "He thinks he is soooo great," Icarus muttered. "But I'll prove that I'm more worthy of Adriadne's breakfast sandwiches than Theseus ever could be," he told himself. But how? Icarus needed his dad's help.

"Uh, Dad?" he said that night in their musty cell tower.

"What is it, Son?" replied Daedalus.

"So there's this girl, and ..."

"Say no more," interrupted his dad. "I'm on it!"

Daedalus had been planning their escape. He built two amazing sets of human-size wings from feathers and wax. "One for you and one for me," he said. "But listen, Son. Don't fly too high, because the hot sun will melt the wax, and the wings will fall apart. And don't fly too low, because the sea will ruin the feathers."

"Got it," said Icarus. But he was already imagining soaring high above Adriadne and Theseus. Despite his dad's warnings, that's exactly what Icarus did. He flew too high to the sun.

"Noooooo! Yo Adriadne!"

Reread the passage. Follow the directions below.

1. What did Daedalus warn Icarus not to do? **Circle** a sentence that shows descriptive details from the story.

2. Why did Icarus fly too close to the sun? **Draw a box** around a sentence that shows how Icarus's character is developed.

3. **Underline** a transition word that shows how one event led to another.

4. **Write** one of the adjectives on the line.

_____

Name _____

| disposed | eavesdropping | fortitude | infinite |
| retaliation | rigors | stoop | undaunted |

Finish each sentence using the vocabulary word provided.

1. **(eavesdropping)** The little boy learned _____
   _____.

2. **(disposed)** If you enjoy volunteering at an animal shelter, _____
   _____.

3. **(fortitude)** It takes a lot of _____
   _____.

4. **(retaliation)** He thought his teammates were being unfair, _____
   _____.

5. **(rigors)** The travelers were worried _____
   _____.

6. **(stoop)** The sisters _____
   _____.

7. **(undaunted)** The girl knew the class would be difficult, _____
   _____.

8. **(infinite)** There seems to be _____
   _____.

Name _____

Read the selection. Complete the cause and effect graphic organizer.

Setting

Event	**Character's Reaction**

Event	**Character's Reaction**

Event	**Character's Reaction**

Name _____

Read the passage. Use the make, confirm, and revise predictions strategy to check your understanding as you read.

Following a Star

	Henry walked carefully through the dark woods. He wished he could
11	progress faster, but he recalled his mother's words, haste makes waste.
22	It would be dangerous to draw attention to himself. The woods were not
35	a safe place for a runaway slave. Nowhere was. His only hope was to
49	travel safely on the Underground Railroad to Canada and freedom. Each
60	home on the line would provide protection from those who would whip or
73	imprison him—or worse—if they caught him.
81	Suddenly, a twig snapped nearby, and Henry jumped. "Oh, no!" he
92	thought, his heart pounding within his chest. He squeezed his eyes shut
104	tight and told himself, "A coward dies a thousand deaths; a brave man
117	dies but once." He turned around, anticipating an angry slave catcher, but
129	instead he saw the worried but friendly face of a boy not much older than
144	himself. "I thought..."
147	"Shh!" the boy hushed Henry, then led him to a large oak.
159	Next to the tree was a woman who stood just a little taller than Henry.
174	He didn't need to see her clearly to know that this figure was the renowned
189	Harriet Tubman, the former slave who had guided so many other slaves to
202	freedom. She was holding a folded sheet of paper in her hand.
214	"I was told that this letter is a warning to folks that you are an escaped
230	slave," Harriet told Henry quietly. "I will tell you how to make your way
244	along the Underground Railroad."
248	Then in a calm voice, Tubman explained how to get to the first station.
262	"Look for a lit lantern hanging outside a home." She reminded Henry that
275	along with those who would help him, there were also those who could
288	destroy him—wild animals and people.
294	"Mrs. Tubman, please take me with you!" Henry blurted out.

Name _____

"Hush up! I'm sorry, Henry," Harriet Tubman said quietly, glancing at the letter in her hand. Harriet knew that escorting Henry along with the other boy, Timothy, would only put him—and them—in even more danger. "You've got to find it in you to be brave."

"But how will I know which direction to go in?" Henry asked.

"Follow the North Star, and always be remembering, stay alert, and understand that your very life depends on your actions. Didn't your mama ever tell you danger foreseen is half avoided?"

Henry thanked Harriet Tubman and began his journey. He knew he couldn't stay in the woods much longer. He needed a clear view of the sky so he could see the North Star.

Dear Neighbors—
Our slave Henry escaped. We believe he may be traveling with Harriet Tubman. Please be on the alert and

As Henry moved closer to the edge of the woods, the moonlight came down on the trees. It created shadows that turned the trees into snarling dogs and men with sticks and ropes. The images filled Henry with a twisting fear. Thinking about the punishments he would face if he were captured terrified him. He began to wonder if he should turn back and return to the plantation. He might still receive a beating, but it would be nothing like what would happen if he were captured.

Still, life at the plantation was very hard. Although he was just a teenager, Henry worked six long days a week, picking cotton under the boiling sun. There he belonged to the master and could be sold at any time.

Unsure of what to do, Henry hung his head, and with a heavy sigh he thought of something else his mama used to say, nothing ventured, nothing gained. Henry had the experience of being a slave his whole life, and he knew that he just HAD to be free!

Henry looked up at the sky and searched until he found the North Star shining down on him like a ray of promise. Fortune favors the bold, thought Henry, and he took off to follow the North Star to freedom.

Name _____

A. Reread the passage and answer the questions.

1. Early in the story, what happens when Henry hears a twig snap? Why?

_____

_____

2. What causes Harriet Tubman to refuse to take Henry with her?

_____

_____

3. In the text in the middle of the second page, how do the shadows in the woods affect Henry after he leaves Harriet Tubman? What does he start to think he should do?

_____

_____

_____

4. In the last two paragraphs, what does Henry remember? What effect do these memories have on him?

_____

_____

_____

B. Work with a partner. Read the passage aloud. Pay attention to expression. Stop after one minute. Fill out the chart.

	Words Read	–	Number of Errors	=	Words Correct Score
First Read		–		=	
Second Read		–		=	

Name _____

The Strength to Speak Out

"Rebecca's been gone for what feels like ten years, Pa, but it is still 1838," Mrs. Miller told her husband.

Mr. Miller responded, "Be strong, dear. She has an important mission. Here, a letter came for you today. Read it aloud."

Mrs. Miller excitedly began reading: "My Dear Mama, I miss you and Papa so. Please, don't fret, for I am safe and well. I have listened to powerful speakers at the abolitionist meeting in Pennsylvania Hall. Angelina Grimké Weld spoke with fervor about the evils of slavery. She urged us all to join together against the shame of our nation. Mama, would you believe that even I took the stage and spoke to our fellow abolitionists? It is true, Mama. Mrs. Weld took my hands, looked in my eyes, and said, 'Rebecca Miller, stand up and speak your mind, for yours is a keen mind and your voice is one of courage.' Be proud of me, Mama. I have become the strong woman you had hoped me to be. With love and devotion to you and Papa, Rebecca."

Answer the questions about the text.

1. What text features of historical fiction does the text contain?
   List two.

   _____

   _____

2. What important information about the main character and the
   plot does the letter reveal?

   _____

   _____

   _____

3. How does the use of dialect help you understand the time period?

   _____

   _____

Name _____

Read each passage below. Using context clues to help you, write a definition of each adage or proverb in bold.

1. Henry walked carefully through the dark woods. He wished he could progress faster, but he recalled his mother's words, **haste makes waste**. It would be dangerous to draw attention to himself.

   _____

2. Suddenly, a twig snapped nearby, and Henry jumped. "Oh, no!" he thought, his heart pounding within his chest. He squeezed his eyes shut tight and told himself, "**A coward dies a thousand deaths; a brave man dies but once**." He turned around, anticipating an angry slave catcher, but instead he saw the worried but friendly face of a boy not much older than himself.

   _____

   _____

3. "Follow the North Star, and always be remembering, stay alert, and understand that your very life depends on your actions. Didn't your mama ever tell you **danger foreseen is half avoided**?"

   _____

   _____

4. Unsure of what to do, Henry hung his head, and with a heavy sigh he thought of something else his mama used to say, **nothing ventured, nothing gained**. Henry had the experience of being a slave his whole life, and he knew that he just HAD to be free!

   _____

5. Henry looked up at the sky and searched until he found the North Star shining down on him like a ray of promise. **Fortune favors the bold**, thought Henry, and he took off to follow the North Star to freedom.

   _____

Name _____

> *bāzār* in Persian means "market"
>
> *iglu* in Inuit means "house"
>
> *kruisen* in Dutch means "to cross"
>
> *plat* in French means "flat"
>
> *pudelhund* in German means "to splash about" plus "dog"

Read each sentence. The word in bold has an origin in a language other than English. Find the related word in the box and write the word and its meaning on the line.

1. The **igloo** kept the family warm even in extremely cold weather.

   _____

2. Our family took a **cruise** down the river during spring break.

   _____

3. We bought several gifts at the winter **bazaar**.

   _____

4. My **poodle** loves to play at the dog park.

   _____

5. After climbing the steep hills, we were glad to reach a **plateau** that extended for miles.

   _____

Name

A. Read the draft model. Use the questions that follow the draft to help you think about how you can add strong, vivid words to help readers visualize the setting and the characters.

Draft Model

Song desperately looked for her sister, but the forest hid her well. Song called out her sister's name. The only answer was the sound of an owl. Song walked carefully through the trees.

---

1. What strong verbs could you use to describe how Song looks and sounds as she searches and calls out?

2. What vivid words could you use to help readers visualize the forest and understand what Song feels?

3. How do you want the sound of the owl to affect readers? What specific words could help you describe the owl's sound to get that effect?

B. Now revise the draft by adding strong, vivid words that will help readers better visualize the setting and the action and to understand how Song is feeling.

_____

_____

_____

_____

_____

_____

_____

Name _____

The student who wrote the paragraphs below used details from two different sources to respond to the prompt: *Imagine that the letter Elijah carried was from a slave to Mrs. Holton. In the letter, explain that Mrs. Holton's husband had been whipped badly but then flew to freedom as in the folktale.*

Dear Emeline,

   I must tell you some bad news about John. He was whipped hard. So hard. And for what? Mr. Tillman thought he stole his gold, and everybody knows John didn't steal that gold. Your John is a good man. He wouldn't steal anything. But Tillman whipped him so hard he dropped straight to the ground like he was a puppet and his strings got cut. I went over to help him, but he was out cold—not breathing. I was worried he wasn't gonna make it.

   But Emeline, I have good news, too. Because just when we all thought John wasn't gonna make it, up came a man. A magic man named Toby. And this Toby raised his arms above John and spoke magic words. He said, "Kum ...yali, kum buba tambe." Then John rose up and soared to freedom. To freedom, Emeline! So don't you worry about John. He is with the ones who fly. He is strong and free.

   Hope his story finds you safe.

Esther

Reread the passage. Follow the directions below.

1. What happened to Mrs. Holton's husband? **Circle** a sentence that shows the development of events.

2. **Draw a box** around a sentence that shows an example of strong, descriptive word choice.

3. **Underline** a transitional phrase that shows how one event led to another.

4. **Write** an example of a demonstrative adjective and an article on the line.

_____

Name _____

inefficient	nutrients	industrial	manipulation
modification	mutated	sparse	surplus

**Write a complete sentence to answer each question below.
In your answer, use the vocabulary word in bold.**

1. What might be **sparse** on a dark winter day?

   _____

2. Why do living creatures need **nutrients**?

   _____

3. What is an **inefficient** way to clear a lawn of fallen leaves?

   _____

4. What might be different about a flower that has **mutated** genes?

   _____

5. What is something that is made by using **industrial** technology?

   _____

6. In which of your school subjects do you use **manipulation**
   of numbers?

   _____

7. What would you do if you had a **surplus** of money?

   _____

8. Why might you make a **modification** to a jacket?

   _____

Name _____

Read the selection. Complete the cause and effect graphic organizer.

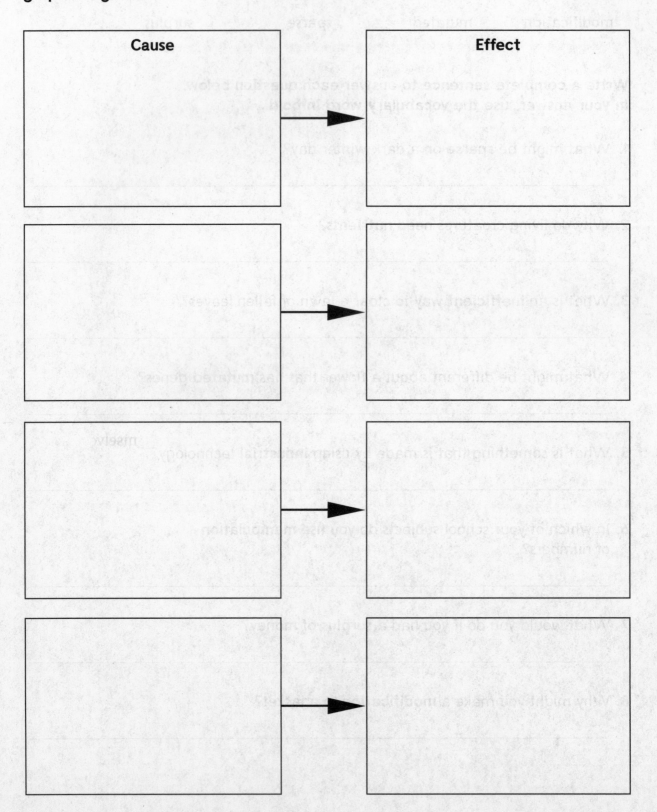

Cause	Effect

Name _____

Read the passage. Use the reread strategy to check your understanding as you read.

Something to Write On, Please

16	Paper is so common today that it is hard to think of living without it. Yet for thousands of years before paper was invented, that is just what people
29	did. In spite of this hardship, people managed over the centuries to come
42	up with a great variety of materials upon which to record their ideas.
55	The earliest writing material used by humans was the wall of a cave.
68	While not much is known about prehistoric writing, one thing is sure.
80	Writing on the wall of a cave could not be moved. To read it, a person
96	would have had to come to it. In a time when the only way to get from one
114	place to another was to walk, cave writers did not have a wide audience.

Stone and Papyrus — 128

131	Much of the early writing of the Egyptians was hieroglyphics, which
142	means picture symbols. The ancient Egyptians carved their writing into the
153	stone of temples or monuments. Because of where the writing was done,
165	the words were made to be as permanent as the buildings themselves.
177	Later the Egyptians made an early paper-like material called *papyrus*.
187	This is the word from which *paper* gets its name. Papyrus was named after
201	a kind of marsh grass growing around the Nile River called papyrus. To
214	make papyrus paper, the Egyptians cut thin strips of grass and soaked them
227	in water. Soaking the strips softened them. To make a flat surface, they
240	laid the strips at right angles to each other and pounded them into a thin
255	sheet. The heat of the sun dried and stiffened the sheets. Dried papyrus
268	was a much lighter substance than stone. It could easily be carried from
281	place to place in rolled sheets called scrolls.

Name _____

Clay Tablets

Near Egypt and about the same time, the ancient Mesopotamians made a form of writing called *cuneiform,* or wedge-shaped writing. Like the Egyptians, the Mesopotamians used materials from their rivers to make writing materials. The end of a reed made a wedge-shaped impression in the wet clay. The drying of the clay made the writing harden and become permanent. But it could still be carried from one place to another.

In fact, some historians think that one of the earliest uses of writing in Mesopotamia was to note lists of goods. These lists were sent along with the goods when they were shipped. Because the writing on the dry clay could not be changed, if something was missing from the shipment, the person receiving it would know!

Ts'ai Lun's Secret Formula

The first person we know of to make something like the paper we use today was a person named Ts'ai Lun. He worked in the Chinese Imperial Court and lived over 1,900 years ago. At that time, books in China were made of bamboo, tortoise shell, and other things that were quite heavy. Silk was also used to make books, but it made them costly. Unhappy with these materials, Lun set out to find something more convenient to write on.

He started by soaking pieces of bark and other plant parts in water. Once the water helped to soften the fibers, Lun pounded them with a wooden tool. After the soaking and pounding, the fibers became thin and threadlike. Using a sieve, Lun carefully separated the threads from the mixture. When the threads were pressed and dried together, they formed thin sheets that one could write on.

Going Paperless?

The amount of paper we use today adds up to a lot of chopped down trees. One paper innovation in recent years has been the use of renewable plant fibers such as bamboo. Bamboo grows fast, while trees take a long time to grow. Now that we use computers to write with, one day, we may not require paper at all!

Name_____

A. Reread the passage and answer the questions.

1. What did Egyptians do to cause papyrus to become a flat
   surface that could be used for writing?

   _____

   _____

2. What was an effect of the Egyptians carving their writing into
   the stone of temples and monuments?

   _____

   _____

3. Look at paragraph 2 on the second page of the passage. What
   was the effect of having lists of goods that were permanently
   written on dry clay? What signal word helps you understand
   this cause and effect relationship?

   _____

   _____

4. What caused the plant fibers that Ts'ai Lun worked with to
   become thin and threadlike?

   _____

   _____

**B. Work with a partner. Read the passage aloud. Pay attention
to rate and accuracy. Stop after one minute. Fill out the chart.**

	Words Read	–	Number of Errors	=	Words Correct Score
First Read		–		=	
Second Read		–		=	

Name _____

The Abacus: Oldest Counting Machine

For thousands of years, the abacus has been used as a counting machine. In many cultures, merchants who traded goods used the wooden beads of the abacus to count goods they bought and sold. They also used the abacus to figure out how much the multiples of their goods would cost. Historians believe that the simplest abacuses probably involved drawing lines in the sand to represent units, such as 100s and 1000s. Small pebbles were used to represent numbers within those units. With the development of number notation, the abacus lost popularity in Europe. However, people in many parts of the world use it to this day.

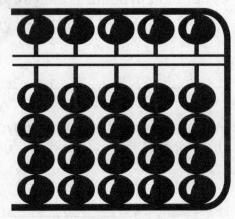

Wooden beads on an abacus were used to count units. Their value depended on the column and position (up or down).

Answer the questions about the text.

1. List two features of expository text that this text contains.

   _____

   _____

2. Besides providing the topic, what does the heading tell you?

   _____

   _____

3. What information in the text is supported by the diagram
   and caption?

   _____

   _____

Name _____

Read each passage below. Determine the cause-and-effect relationship described in each. Write the missing cause or effect on the line provided. Then, thinking about the cause and effect, define the word in bold in each passage.

1. To make papyrus paper, the Egyptians cut thin strips of grass and soaked them in water. Soaking the strips softened them. To make a flat surface, they laid the strips at right angles to each other and **pounded** them into a thin sheet.

   cause: _____

   effect: making papyrus paper with a flat surface

   definition of **pounded**: _____

2. The end of a reed made a wedge-shaped **impression** in the wet clay.

   cause: end of reed pushed into clay

   effect: _____

   definition of **impression**: _____

3. The drying of the clay made the writing harden and become **permanent**.

   cause: drying of the clay

   effect: _____

   definition of **permanent**: _____

4. Silk was also used to make books, but it made them **costly**.

   cause: using silk, an expensive material, to make books

   effect: _____

   definition of **costly**: _____

Name _____

benefit	transport	structure	factory
audience	manufacture	reflection	beneficial
exported	reflex	destruction	audio

A. Read the words in the box above. Sort them based on their Latin roots. Write each word in the correct column.

aud	*bene*	*flect/flex*	*port*	*struct*	*fac/fact*
_____	_____	_____	_____	_____	_____
_____	_____	_____	_____	_____	_____

Latin Roots and their Meanings

- *aud* means "hear"
- *flect* and *flex* mean "bend"
- *struct* means "build"

- *bene* and *bon* mean "good"
- *port* means "carry"
- *fac* and *fact* mean "make" or "do"

B. Circle the word with the Latin root in each sentence. Use the root meanings above and your knowledge of word parts to determine the meaning of the word. Then write the meaning on the line.

1. Cars were sent around the construction site. _____

2. People filled the auditorium before the show. _____

3. At the meet, the gymnasts showed how flexible they are. _____

4. This rug was imported from India. _____

Name _____

A. Read the draft model. Use the questions that follow the draft to help you think about how to best organize the text so that ideas are logically connected.

Draft Model

The washing machine was a very important invention. It made life easier for many people. Before, clothes were washed by hand. This took hours. Now washing machines could do most of the work.

---

1. What signal words can you insert to highlight cause-and-effect relationships?

2. How could sentences be revised or rearranged to clearly link causes and effects?

3. What words or phrases can you use to signal the order of events?

B. Now revise the draft by adding signal words that will help the reader understand the order of events and the relationships between ideas.

_____

_____

_____

_____

_____

_____

_____

_____

_____

Name _____

The student who wrote the paragraphs below used details from two different sources to answer the question: *What innovations have people made in working with plants to meet their needs?*

For thousands of years, people have come up with innovative ways to work with plants to meet their needs. For example, the Indians of Mesoamerica began growing food crops when the animals they hunted grew scarce. First, they planted squash, gourds, and peppers. Then they created a nutritious new food source called maize. To grow maize, they created a better farming system in which different crops are planted in a field at the same time. Not only was the variety of plants good for the soil, it was good for a person's diet.

People have also used plants to treat illnesses. For example, honey could be put on cuts, and the spice coriander could ease upset stomachs. In fact, many medicines today come from plants. But when the plant sources became too rare or expensive, researchers had to get creative. They modified the natural compounds in plants to make a synthetic version. For example, aspirin comes from compounds in the bark of a willow tree.

Innovations that Mesoamericans and medical researchers made have affected people all over the world.

Reread the passage. Follow the directions below.

1. What is the topic of this writing sample? **Circle** a sentence that shows the thesis statement.

2. In what innovative ways did researchers work with plants? **Draw a box** around a sentence that shows details to support the topic.

3. When did Mesoamericans create maize? **Underline** words that show the order in which the details and facts happened.

4. **Write** a comparative adjective on the line.

_____

Name _____

| colleagues | conservatively | deduction | drones |
| galaxy | sustain | ultimately | verify |

Finish each sentence using the vocabulary word provided.

1. **(verify)** Please recheck your facts _____
_____.

2. **(deduction)** The scientist was _____
_____.

3. **(drones)** In the next room, _____
_____.

4. **(galaxy)** There are many _____
_____.

5. **(colleagues)** We weren't sure what to do, _____
_____.

6. **(conservatively)** I think that we can _____
_____.

7. **(sustain)** Most plants and animals need _____
_____.

8. **(ultimately)** After a long discussion, _____
_____.

Name _____

Read the selection. Complete the sequence graphic organizer.

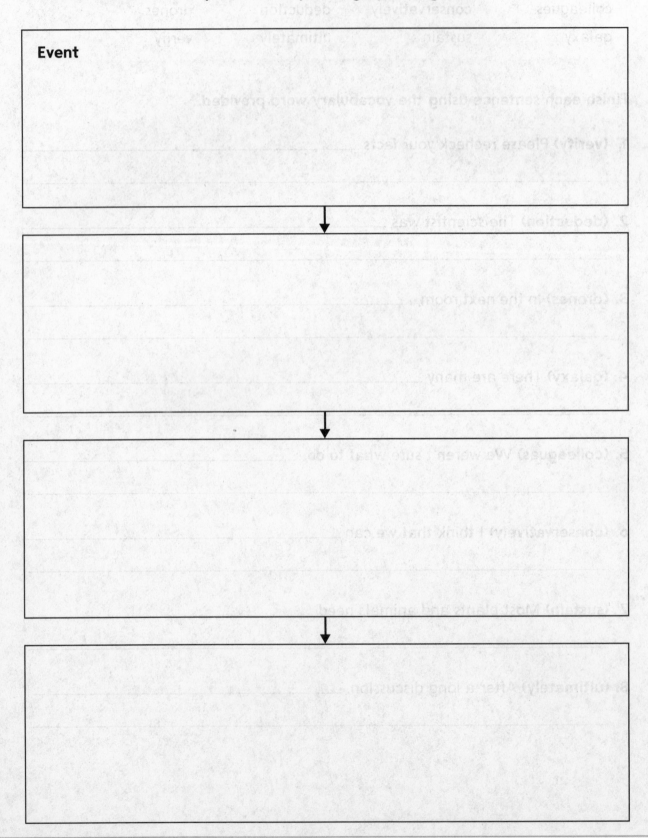

Event

Name _____

Read the passage. Use the reread strategy to check your understanding as you read.

Satellites Take Archeology to New Heights

10	Like detectives in hot pursuit of evidence, archeologists hunt for
22	information that is often hidden. They dig for clues about ancient people
34	whose cultures have vanished and are gone from view. For many years,
45	archeologists used simple tools such as hand shovels and sifters. They
56	carefully removed sand and dirt from relics. They hoped these objects
67	from the past would unlock the mysteries of ancient civilizations. Now
77	a new tool has transformed archeology. Satellite images reveal secrets
90	hidden below the earth. They show in a picture what the human eye
	sometimes cannot see.
93	**Going High-Tech**
95	In 2000 archeologist Sarah Parcak began searching for traces of ancient
106	villages in Egypt. She knew that buildings could have been buried in the
119	Nile River floodplain. The shifting desert sands could have covered over
130	whole settlements. However, Parcak wanted to try a high-tech approach
140	to help pinpoint, or narrow down, possible sites. Parcak was familiar with
152	satellite imaging for small projects. She wanted to apply it more broadly
164	across Egypt.
166	In 2010 Parcak and her team had two sets of satellite imaging to look
180	at. For over a year, they studied and compared both sets. Parcak found that
194	the most revealing pictures were taken during late winter when the soil
206	was wet. Parcak and her team could see where the buildings were. The
219	ancient underground buildings were made of mud brick. When the buried
230	walls were wet, the images showed differences between the soil above the
242	walls and the soil next to them. Now the team had clues, a starting point.

Name _____

Proof on the Ground

In the satellite pictures, Parcak and the team could easily see the sites of pyramids that were above the ground. They compared those images with the outlines of similar structures that were underground and found more pyramids. The satellite pictures also revealed the layout of an underground city. Using the images, Parcak and her team were able to create a map of Tanis, an ancient Egyptian capital.

The archeologists knew they would have to prove their theories. In 2011 Parcak's satellite technology pinpointed where to dig. Partnering with a group of French archeologists, Parcak's team explored the Tanis site. They uncovered a house right where the satellite picture had shown it would be. The team also did a trial dig for pyramids. They found two. The pyramids were exactly where the pictures showed they should be. "They found an almost 100% correlation between what we see on the imagery and what we see on the ground," Parcak said.

In total, the high-tech research has uncovered 17 buried pyramids, 1,000 tombs, and 3,000 settlements. Parcak's idea of using satellite technology has paid off. She is eager to see how this technology will reveal more about life in ancient Egypt.

Pictures of the earth taken from satellites can help archeologists.

Further Exploration

Archeologists predict there will be many more uses for satellite technology. Today the Egyptian government uses satellite imaging to protect their ancient sites. If there is looting, the authorities can be alerted. This may help keep down such theft in the tombs. Archeologists can also use satellites to study sites in war-torn countries, where ground visits are difficult. Another archeologist has learned how ancient water canals helped the Mayans farm.

Satellites were first developed in connection with space exploration. They are also helping us get to know our own planet better. Sometimes you have to step back to see the big picture.

A. Reread the passage and answer the questions.

1. What tools did archeologists use for many years to find relics?
   What is a new tool? What time word signals the sequence?

   _____

   _____

2. What signal words tell you how long Parcak and her team
   worked with the satellite images of the Nile floodplain? What
   did the team of archeologists do with the images?

   _____

   _____

3. What did the archeologists do right before they started digging
   in 2011?

   _____

   _____

4. How many years after Parcak began searching for ancient
   villages did she and her team begin digging at the site of Tanis?
   How do you know?

   _____

   _____

**B. Work with a partner. Read the passage aloud. Pay attention
to expression. Stop after one minute. Fill out the chart.**

	Words Read	–	Number of Errors	=	Words Correct Score
First Read		–		=	
Second Read		–		=	

Name _____

Shipwreck Located Below Lake Ontario

For Jim Kennard, the search for the 18th-century British warship *HMS Ontario* lasted 35 years. In 2008, Kennard teamed up with Dan Scoville, and the two men used sonar, or sound, technology to locate the shipwreck in Lake Ontario. But underwater divers could not reach it, because the ship lay 500 feet below the surface. Instead, the men used an underwater remotely operated vehicle (ROV) that Scoville developed to explore and confirm the identity of the ship. The ROV has high-intensity lighting and cameras that take images of shipwrecks. The images showed a large sailing ship. Finally, Kennard had found the *HMS Ontario*.

The *HMS Ontario* was 24.5 meters long (over 80 feet) with masts almost as tall as the length of the ship.

Answer the questions about the text.

1. How is the information in the text organized? How does it help you?

_____

_____

2. What inventions helped Kennard and Scoville make their discovery?

_____

3. What part of the process helped confirm the identity of the ship?

_____

_____

4. What technical information do the diagram and its caption provide?

_____

_____

Name _____

**Read each passage. Underline the context clues that define or
restate the meaning of the word in bold. Write the definition
of the word. Then use the word in a sentence of your own.**

1. Like detectives in **pursuit** of evidence, archeologists hunt for clues.

   Definition: _____

   Sentence: _____

   _____

2. They dig for clues about ancient people whose cultures have
   vanished and are gone from view.

   Definition: _____

   Sentence: _____

   _____

3. They carefully removed dirt from **relics**. They hoped these objects
   from the past would unlock the mysteries of ancient civilizations.

   Definition: _____

   Sentence: _____

   _____

4. Satellite **images** reveal secrets hidden below the earth. They show
   in a picture what the human eye sometimes cannot see.

   Definition: _____

   Sentence: _____

   _____

5. However, Parcak wanted to **pinpoint**, or narrow down, possible sites.

   Definition: _____

   Sentence: _____

Name _____

A. Add the word parts to create a word with a Greek root. Write the word. Then circle the word below that has the same Greek root.

1. aero + space = _____

   automated   aerodynamic   alleviate

2. bio + graph + y = _____

   autograph   bizarre   microwave

3. photo + synthesis = _____

   philosophy   telephoto   program

4. psych + ologist = _____

   pathetic   polar   psychic

5. para + graph = _____

   grapes   invite   graphic

B. Complete each sentence with a word from the box. Use the meanings of Greek roots to help you.

| aerobic   psychology   photocopy   photographer |

6. He made a _____ of his passport before he left.

7. Swimming is considered an excellent _____ activity.

8. A _____ uses a camera to take pictures.

9. In a _____ class, students learn about the mind.

Name_____

A. Read the draft model. Use the questions that follow the draft to help you think about how to strengthen the organization of the paragraph's main idea and supporting details.

Draft Model

I think we should visit the moon again. The last time a human walked on the moon was in 1972. Since that time, there have been many advances in technology.

---

1. What words or phrases could you add to make the topic sentence clearer?

2. How could the second sentence be revised to help it better support the topic sentence?

3. What points could be added to help strengthen the ideas in the last sentence and to link ideas to the topic? What transitions could be used?

4. What sentence could you add to the end to make the reader want to read the next paragraph?

B. Now revise the draft by creating a stronger topic sentence and by giving stronger, more specific support for the topic.

_____

_____

_____

_____

_____

_____

_____

Name _____

The student who wrote the paragraphs below used details from two different sources to answer the question: *How is Anisisbro from* Excursion to Mars *similar to the spectrometer described in "Planet Hunter"?*

Even though Anisisbro is a fictional robot from the story *Excursion to Mars*, it is similar to the spectrometer described in "Planet Hunter."

One way Anisisbro and the spectrometer are similar is that they are both inventions that led to new discoveries. In *Excursion to Mars*, a colony's air supply became contaminated, and no human could figure out the contamination without getting sick. Since Anisisbro was a robot, it could find the source of the contamination without becoming contaminated itself. In "Planet Hunter," the author explains that the spectrometer discovers new planets that can't be seen by a telescope.

Another way the two inventions are similar is in how they work. In *Excursion to Mars*, Anisisbro is described as having a "particle analyzer." This is exactly how a spectrometer works. It separates starlight into a spectrum of visible colors. By analyzing the different-color wavelengths, scientists can tell whether a star is moving toward Earth or away from Earth, and therefore, how a planet's gravitational pull is affecting that star.

Finally, these inventions are similar in what they accomplished and how they worked—and like most scientific technologies, they are fascinating!

Reread the passage. Follow the directions below.

1. **Circle** a sentence that shows the thesis statement.

2. **Draw a box** around strong sentences that help explain the topic.

3. **Underline** the sequence word that concludes the topic.

4. **Write** a comparative adjective on the line and explain what it compares.

_____

_____

Name _____

catastrophic	elevating	computations	subsequently
magnetic	obsolete	application	deployed

**Write a complete sentence to answer each question below.
In your answer, use the vocabulary word in bold.**

1. Why might you use something **magnetic**?

    _____

2. What kind of homework usually involves **computations**?

    _____

3. What is something you would describe as **catastrophic**?

    _____

4. Why might an ambulance be **deployed**?

    _____

    _____

5. If you were injured, what might you **subsequently** do?

    _____

6. What is a typical **application** for a hammer?

    _____

7. Why would you call an old typewriter an **obsolete** writing tool?

    _____

8. What might be one reason for **elevating** a sign?

    _____

Name _____

Read the selection. Complete the author's point of view graphic organizer.

Details	Author's Point of View

Name _____

Read the passage. Use the summarize strategy to check your understanding.

Hurtling Through Space from Home

	If you've ever wondered what it's like to travel in space, now you can
14	find out. Space hobbyists have written some amazing computer programs.
24	Some let you see what's out there as if you were at a planetarium. Other
39	programs let you soar through the universe from home like an astronaut.
51	From the world's largest map to flight simulations, this space exploration
62	can be a lot of fun. Virtual space flights are not just for kids and teenagers.
78	Many computer astronauts are adults. They want to know how it feels to
91	guide a spacecraft through our vast solar system.

99	**Many Ways to Learn with Technology**

105	Have you ever looked in awe at the enormous, brightly lit night sky?
118	You can now get a closer look without going to a planetarium. Computer
131	programs are available to the public using data from real orbiters and
143	telescopes. The Sloan Digital Sky Survey is an effort to create a map of
157	the universe. Its creators have identified hundreds of millions of objects.
168	Anyone with a computer can see images and data from the survey by
181	logging onto SkyServer. Navigation tools take you on a journey through
192	the night sky. It would be easy to get lost out in the universe. SkyServer
207	provides games and projects to keep computer astronauts on course.
217	Since 2009 NASA and Microsoft have worked together to make
227	planetary images and data available to the public. The result is the
239	WorldWide Telescope. Its creators call it "the world's best telescope."
249	This online tool gathers information from telescopes and observatories
258	throughout the world. Guided tours take you on a space journey billions of
271	years into the past. One feature even lets you see into the future. You can
286	view the planets' positions from any place on Earth at any time.

Name _____

Stellarium is an easy-to-use astronomy program. You can observe the sun, moon, planets, and stars just as you might at a planetarium. Zoom in to find the names of objects in the sky. Look at the universe from anywhere, not just gazing up from Earth. To visit Jupiter, simply type in the planet's name. The program shoots you across the night sky. You can enjoy the wonder at close range.

Celestia is another piece of free software that provides the experience of exploring our galaxy. You will not be in a cockpit for this virtual adventure. This program is also more like visiting a planetarium. However, you may plot locations in the solar system and travel between planets. There is an easy "Go To" feature. Just pick a planet or star you wish to zoom in on. You see stars, planets, and moons pass by until you get where you want to go.

Virtual Orbiting

Bruce Irving is one of NASA's Solar System Ambassadors. He is a skillful author and teacher of computer space explorers. His free, online books help people to use Dr. Martin Schweiger's space simulation program called Orbiter. You can experience a ride in a spaceship by using pre-recorded flights. Launch and re-entry modeling make for realistic space travel. Later on, you can learn how to plan your own trip to Mars. Or you can see Jupiter from your virtual cockpit. Orbiter has enough levels of learning to challenge even advanced users.

It's easy to get interested in space exploration and flight simulation. Computer programs have paved the way for many people of all ages to experience space. Willing scientists and computer experts have made the thrill of spaceflight possible for everyone.

Graphics such as this—the cockpit of the Orbiter's Delta-glider vehicle— add to the realism of space-flight simulation.

Simulations Require Training

Spaceflight simulation demands some learning before you can do much more than take a demonstration ride. As you can see from looking at the virtual cockpit in the demo model, experiencing simulations of launches of your own will require some tutorial work.

Name _____

A. Reread the passage and answer the questions.

1. What detail does the author include about what you can do
   using the WorldWide Telescope?

   _____

   _____

2. What details does the author include about what you can do
   with the program Celestia?

   _____

   _____

3. What words that the author uses to describe Stellarium give
   you evidence about the author's view of the program?

   _____

   _____

4. How would you describe the author's point of view about
   computer programs that simulate space exploration?

   _____

   _____

   _____

**B. Work with a partner. Read the passage aloud. Pay attention
to rate and accuracy. Stop after one minute. Fill out the chart.**

	Words Read	–	Number of Errors	=	Words Correct Score
First Read		–		=	
Second Read		–		=	

Name _____

NASA's Robotic Lander

Picture a "robot" spacecraft landing on a faraway planet. NASA is testing just such a robotic lander to explore the moon and other bodies in space. "Mighty Eagle," the first lander of this type, is a 700-pound, three-legged craft, and is four feet tall and eight feet wide. During tests in 2011, the lander reached an altitude of 100 feet, hovered a while, and then landed safely. An on-board pre-programmed computer guides "Mighty Eagle," our newest advance in space exploration.

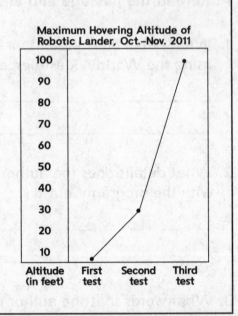

Maximum Hovering Altitude of Robotic Lander, Oct.–Nov. 2011

Answer the questions about the text.

1. How do you know this is expository text?

   _____

   _____

2. What text features does this text include?

   _____

3. Based on the information in the text, is the heading a strong one? Why or why not?

   _____

   _____

4. What information does the line graph provide?

   _____

Name _____

Read each sentence. Then explain how the tone of the sentence would change if the words in bold were replaced with the words in parentheses.

1. Other programs let you **soar** through the universe from home like an astronaut. (fly)

   _____

   _____

2. From the world's largest map to flight simulations, this space **exploration** can be a lot of fun. (research)

   _____

   _____

3. They want to know how it feels to guide a spacecraft through our **vast** solar system. (big)

   _____

   _____

4. You can enjoy the **wonder** at close range. (impressive sight)

   _____

   _____

5. Celestia is another piece of free software that provides the **experience** of exploring our galaxy. (activity)

   _____

   _____

6. Bruce Irving is one of NASA's Solar System **Ambassadors**. (Representatives)

   _____

   _____

Name _____

A. Read each sentence and look for words with the suffix *-ive, -age,* or *-ize*. Underline the suffix. Then write the word on the line.

1. I'm glad that my friend could sympathize with my situation. _____

2. We had the advantage of practicing on the stage. _____

3. The live debate between the candidates was explosive. _____

4. Should we organize these drawings by size? _____

5. The passage across the sea seemed like it lasted for ages. _____

B. Read the words in the box. Then sort the words based on their suffixes in the chart below.

| vocalize | wreckage | attractive | creative | emphasize |
| criticize | storage | secretive | percentage | |

-ive	*-age*	*-ize*
_____	_____	_____
_____	_____	_____
_____	_____	_____

Name _____

A. Read the draft model. Use the questions that follow the draft to help you revise the draft by replacing less-precise words with content words about the technical subject.

Draft Model

My favorite piece of new technology is a tablet computer. It has a fast processor and programmable keys. It also has lots of memory.

---

1. What words in the model can be replaced with more precise content words about this new technology?

2. How can you use content words to be more specific about the amount of memory the tablet has?

3. What other content words can you add to the draft? For example, does the tablet have a camera? Does it have any special apps?

B. Now revise the draft by replacing less-precise words with content words.

_____

_____

_____

_____

_____

_____

_____

_____

_____

Name _____

The student who wrote the paragraphs below used details from two different sources to answer the question: *Should Houston, Texas, have been a final destination for one of the shuttles from NASA's space shuttle program?*

"Houston, we have a problem." The problem is that none of the space shuttles from NASA's space shuttle program ended up in Houston, Texas. For 30 years, Johnson Space Center in Houston was home of mission control for the program. The people in that control room—in Houston—helped accomplish some of the greatest missions in space exploration. For example, the space shuttle *Discovery* launched the Hubble Space Telescope, which has allowed astronomers to see deeper into space. The space shuttle *Endeavour* was sent to fix Hubble when it sent back blurry images, and the mission was a success! The images were better. The space shuttles also carried construction materials for International Space Station.

Also, Houston was home for astronauts when they weren't traveling in space. They lived, worked, and raised their families in Houston.

Bringing one of the space shuttles to Houston would have been like bringing it back home. The people who spent decades of their lives working in the program deserved to honor what they worked so hard to achieve.

Reread the passage. Follow the directions below.

1. What are some of the specific accomplishments of the space shuttle program? **Circle** precise language that supports the argument.

2. Why should Houston have been a final destination for one of the space shuttles? **Draw a box** around text evidence that supports the argument.

3. **Underline** the strong conclusion that will lead readers to think about the claim.

4. **Write** a word that is a comparative form of another word on the line.

_____

Name _____

commodity	distribution	dominant	edible
impenetrable	ornate	replenished	significant

Use each pair of vocabulary words in a single sentence.

1. impenetrable, significant

_____

_____

_____

2. commodity, distribution

_____

_____

_____

3. edible, replenished

_____

_____

_____

4. ornate, dominant

_____

_____

_____

Name _____

Read the selection. Complete the main idea and key details graphic organizer.

Main Idea

Detail

Detail

Detail

Name _____

Read the passage. Use the ask and answer questions strategy to check for understanding as you read.

Harnessing the Sun's Energy

14	For as long as people have lived on Earth, they have depended on the sun for the energy they need. Energy from the sun is called solar energy.
28	In ancient times, people were warmed directly by the sun and indirectly
40	by the solar energy stored in wood when they burned it. They used stored
54	solar energy whenever they ate plants or animals that got their energy from
67	plants. Today we use the solar energy stored in oil, coal, and natural gas.
81	All of these are formed over very long periods of time.
92	Because coal, oil, and gas take a long time to form, using them as
106	energy sources has a disadvantage. They cannot be replaced as we use
118	them. Today people are looking for ways to use solar energy directly from
131	sunlight. Solar energy used in this way is called solar power. Because
143	Earth receives light from the sun constantly, direct solar energy is a
155	renewable source of energy.
159	Many ancient people found ways to harness solar power by converting,
170	or turning, sunlight into thermal energy (heat). Greeks and Romans used
181	the sun's reflection on mirrors to light torches. Romans found that using
193	glass windows would capture the sun's warmth. Native Americans built
203	houses into the sides of cliffs. They used the sun's heat from the day for
218	warmth at night. Solar technology is not new. However, we continue to
230	learn ways to harness the sun's power.

	From Light to Electricity
237	
241	Today we also have the technology to turn solar energy into electrical
253	energy (electricity). In 1839 a French scientist by the name of Edmund
265	Becquerel made a breakthrough discovery. He observed that certain
274	materials made electrical current when they absorbed light. In 1905
284	Albert Einstein described the details of this process. Einstein's work was
295	the basis for much progress in solar technology.

Name _____

Convert, Collect, and Store

In the 1950s, American scientists developed a solar cell that could convert the sun's energy into current. One cell did not produce much electricity. Soon the cells were placed into larger units called modules. Then NASA decided to invest in solar energy for space travel. By combining solar modules, they made a more powerful electrical source called an array. NASA first used this technology on their satellite called Vanguard I in 1958.

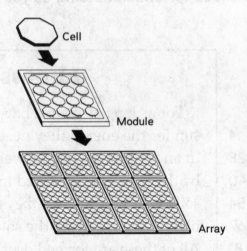

The sun's energy can produce heat and power, but it must somehow be stored for later use. Some electrical power can be stored in batteries. Solar heat can also be captured by collectors and then stored. In 1767 a Swiss scientist developed the first solar collector. A flat plate collector uses black metal plates covered with pieces of glass. The glass heats up as the sun strikes. The heat is then carried by water or air to storage. Collectors are often used for heating homes or water. A focusing collector is used to capture greater heat. In these, a layout of carefully placed mirrors focuses the sunlight. The light goes from a wide area and is concentrated into a small black receiver. These solar furnaces can reach temperatures of up to 2,000 degrees Celsius.

An Available Renewable Energy

Solar power has many advantages. It does not pollute. This resource is free and widely available. The challenge is collecting and storing energy from this source cheaply. Today, more people use solar power in their homes and businesses. Water heaters and collection panels are cutting energy costs. New designs in windows, skylights, and even roof shingles help homeowners use the sun's energy directly.

From ancient people to today, humans have looked for ways to harness our amazing sun. With awareness of the need for renewable, clean energy, looking to the sun just makes sense. The potential for solar power is enormous.

Name _____

A. Reread the passage and answer the questions.

1. Look at the first paragraph. Write two details that support the main idea that people have always depended on the sun for energy.

   _____

   _____

   _____

   _____

2. What is the main idea of the third paragraph?

   _____

   _____

   _____

3. Look at the second paragraph under the heading "Convert, Collect, and Store." What is the main idea of that paragraph? Name one detail that supports this idea.

   _____

   _____

   _____

   _____

B. Work with a partner. Read the passage aloud. Pay attention to rate and accuracy. Stop after one minute. Fill out the chart.

	Words Read	–	Number of Errors	=	Words Correct Score
First Read		–		=	
Second Read		–		=	

Name_____

Lithium: The World's Newest Commodity

Like oil and natural gas that fuel our cars and homes, lithium has become a valuable commodity, or product. It is a light silvery-white metal with high electrical conductivity. Therefore, electronics that require a long battery life, such as laptops and mobile phones, run on lithium. The world's largest supply lies within the salt flats of Chile and Bolivia in South America. Although lithium is a clean energy source, mining for it is dirty work. The precious metal is pumped out of the ground and left to bake in the hot desert sun. It then becomes a yellow greasy liquid that can be used as energy. For some people, the question remains: How much environmental damage will lithium mining cause?

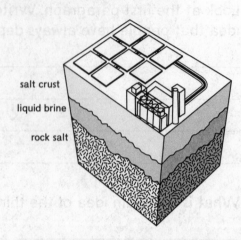

salt crust

liquid brine

rock salt

Lithium from the liquid brine layer is pumped up to the earth's surface.

Answer the questions about the text.

1. What process does the text explain?

_____

_____

2. How do the diagram and caption help you understand this process?

_____

_____

3. Why are some people concerned about lithium mining?

_____

Name _____

Read each sentence. Use the chart below to help you figure out the meaning of each word in bold. Then write the root of each word and a new sentence using that word.

Latin Root	Meaning
flec, flex	bend, break
ology	study or science of
scrib, scrip	write
vert, vers	turn
sign	sign

1. Many ancient people found ways to harness solar power by **converting**, or turning, sunlight into thermal energy (heat).

   root: _____

   sentence: _____

2. Greeks and Romans used the sun's **reflection** on mirrors to light torches.

   root: _____

   sentence: _____

3. Solar **technology** is not new.

   root: _____

   sentence: _____

4. In 1905, Albert Einstein **described** the details of this process.

   root: _____

   sentence: _____

5. New **designs** in windows, skylights, and even roof shingles help homeowners use the sun's energy directly.

   root: _____

   sentence: _____

Name _____

A. Read each word in bold. Then circle the related word with the suffix *-ible* or *-able*.

1. **value**   valuable   valued   remarkable

2. **profit**   professional   profitable   profits

3. **consider**   changeable   considerable   considerate

4. **love**   lovely   adorable   lovable

5. **horror**   horrible   honorable   horrifying

B. Read each clue. Then choose a word from the box that matches it. Write the word on the line and circle the suffix.

reversible	impossible	admirable	predictable	believable
terrible	acceptable	reliable	noticeable	considerable

6. worthy of admiration _____

7. able to be reversed _____

8. capable of being noticed _____

9. able to be believed _____

10. causing terror _____

Name _____

A. Read the draft model. Use the questions that follow the draft to help you think about how to vary sentence length and sentence structure.

Draft Model

We need to protect our water supply. People, animals, and plants will die without it. We should stop pollution.

1. What new details could you add to the first sentence to grab the reader's attention? How could adding this information make the first sentence a compound sentence?

2. How could you make the second sentence shorter to emphasize the point? How could this sentence be reorganized so the subject is not at the beginning?

3. What words, phrases, or clauses could you add to the third sentence to better relate this idea to the other sentences?

B. Now revise the draft by varying the sentence length and structure so that the writing seems more natural and more able to keep the reader's interest.

_____

_____

_____

_____

_____

_____

_____

Name _____

The student who wrote the paragraphs below used details from two different sources to answer the question: *How do the text features support the text in* **The Story of Salt** *and "The Not So Golden Touch"?*

In *The Story of Salt* and "The Not So Golden Touch," the illustrators use pictures to help the reader understand the text. In *The Story of Salt,* for example, the picture of colonists trading goods for salt across continents helps the reader understand that the British tried to control the salt trade. In "The Not So Golden Touch," the reader sees in the pictures that everything the king touches turns to gold.

Sometimes text features can also help the reader figure out information that is not in the text. For example, the picture of the Wieliczka salt mine in *The Story of Salt* suggests that people often visited salt mines as tourists.

Text features can also help the reader understand the meaning of words. The picture of the mummy covered in salt helped me figure out the meaning of the word *preserve.*

Text features of both stories help the reader easily understand the text. *The Story of Salt* includes pictures that give a little more information and help the reader fully understand the meaning of some words.

Reread the passage. Follow the directions below.

1. What are these paragraphs about? **Circle** the sentence that introduces the topic.

2. **Draw a box** around two sentences that show different sentence patterns.

3. **Underline** the strong conclusion that restates the topic sentence and follows logically from the evidence in the paragraphs.

4. **Write** an adverb on the line.

_____

Name _____

agitated	crucial	futile	populous
presumed	smoldering	undiminished	urgency

Write a complete sentence to answer each question below. In your answer, use the vocabulary word in bold.

1. What kind of situation might create an **urgency** to leave a building?

_____

2. What kind of place is a **populous** city? _____

_____

3. If he **presumed** he would do well on the test, what did he believe?

_____

_____

4. Why is it dangerous to pick up a **smoldering** piece of wood?

_____

_____

5. What is something that can cause people to become **agitated**?

_____

6. Why is it **crucial** to learn about safety? _____

_____

7. What is something that can be considered **futile**? _____

_____

8. If a fire is **undiminished**, does it give off less heat than before? _____

_____

Name _____

Read the selection. Complete the cause and effect graphic organizer.

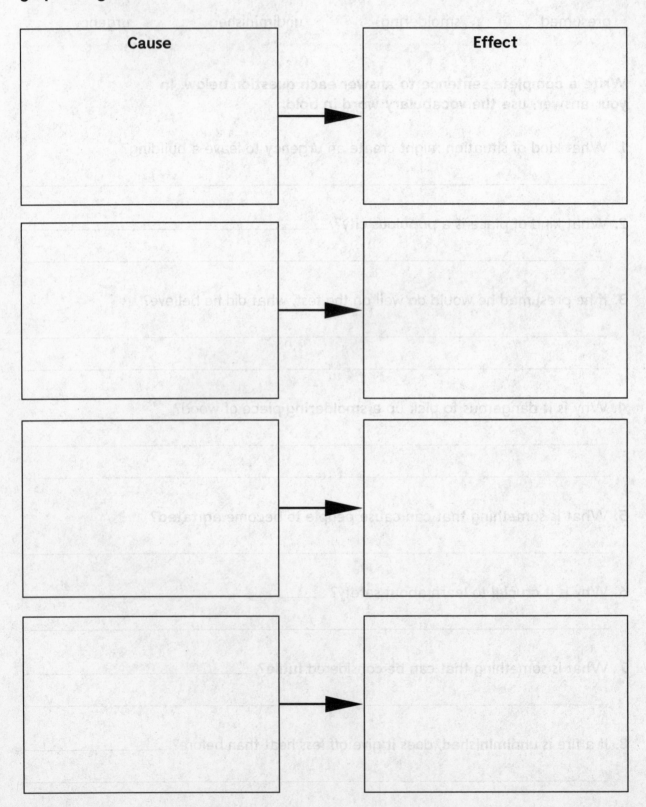

Cause		Effect

Name_____

Read the passage. Use the ask and answer questions strategy to check your understanding as you read.

The Triangle Shirtwaist Fire

	New York City was a booming industrial center in 1911. The garment
12	industry was one of the largest employers in the city at that time.
25	Immigrant women and girls were often the ones who worked in these
37	factories, cutting and sewing fabric for clothing. The garment factories
47	were in great competition. As a result, workers' pay and factory conditions
59	often suffered. It was common for immigrant workers to work in unclean,
71	overcrowded factories.
73	The Triangle Shirtwaist Factory specialized in making a popular
82	women's blouse called the shirtwaist. The Triangle Factory was on the
93	top three floors of the ten-story Asch Building. Nearly 500 of the 600
106	employees were young women and girls. Sewing machines were crowded
116	together with hardly an aisle to walk between them. Cloth scraps littered
128	the floors. Webs of thread and cloth draped over chairs and tables. There
141	was no time for cleanup.
146	At 4:45 P.M. on March 25, 1911, the Triangle Shirtwaist Factory erupted
158	into an uncontrollable blaze. It was the close of a workday. Many were
171	ready to walk out with their coats in hand. It was a cruel fate for the 146
188	people who died, trapped in flames within minutes of their freedom!
199	A tailor on the eighth floor heard the first cry of fire. He and the
214	manager grabbed buckets and began dousing the flames with water. A
225	feast for the hungry fire, long rope lines of shirtwaist garments hung above
238	sewing tables. While the men tossed water on the fire, the rope burned in
252	two. As a result, the flaming blouses fell onto electric sewing machines
264	and wooden tables below. Soon the cloth-filled room was an uncontrolled
275	wildfire.

A Picture Is Worth a Thousand Words

As clouds gather before a storm, the first sparks of flame foreshadowed an unthinkable disaster in New York City. Chaos reigned inside the factory. The workers found exit doors locked. There was only one fire escape. One elevator worked, but for only a short time. Stairwells soon filled with fire. Because they had nowhere to go, the employees faced unwelcome choices.

Sarah Friedman Dworetz worked on the ninth floor that dreadful day. She said in an interview, "There was screaming and shoving and many girls tried to climb over the machine tables." As Sarah waited for the elevator, she saw the flames coming from all sides. "Suddenly I was holding to the sides of the door looking down the elevator shaft with girls screaming and pushing behind me." She reached for the elevator cable and grabbed hold. Sarah slid down the shaft, landing on top of the elevator, unconscious. Other girls followed Sarah, many falling on top of her broken body.

Many other girls tried to escape through the windows. Unfortunately, they were unable to do so. The murderous fire was over in thirty minutes.

In this factory, advice when most needed was least heeded. There had been other fires at the Triangle Factory. Experts had called for more safety measures. In 1909 union workers protested the conditions in a strike. Their suggestions were ignored. The owners were not convicted of a crime, but public outrage did lead to reform. Workers organized, and political leaders took action. Many would say

Horse-drawn fire engine, on its way to the Triangle Shirtwaist Company fire

that the reforms were better late than never. For the women who lost their lives, however, it was too little too late.

Name _____

A. Reread the passage and answer the questions.

1. What caused the low workers' pay and poor working conditions in garment factories in the early 1900s?

   _____

   _____

2. Once the fire began, what was the effect of having cloth, thread, and blouses all over the factory?

   _____

   _____

   _____

3. What caused so many workers to become trapped in the factory?

   _____

   _____

   _____

4. What was the effect of people's outrage about the fire?

   _____

   _____

   _____

B. Work with a partner. Read the passage aloud. Pay attention to intonation and phrasing. Stop after one minute. Fill out the chart.

	Words Read	–	Number of Errors	=	Words Correct Score
First Read		–		=	
Second Read		–		=	

Name_____

Baltimore in Flames

For firefighters at Engine 15 in Baltimore, Maryland, February 7, 1904, seemed like an ordinary Sunday morning. Everything changed at 10:48 A.M. when they received a fire alarm from John Hurst and Company. Soon after the fire engine arrived at the building, a basement fire caused an explosion in the elevator shaft. From there, the fire spread rapidly. For two days, firefighters worked frantically to put out the blaze that swallowed the city. The *New York Times* reported on February 9, 1904, "A territory twelve full city blocks by nine, and extending beyond over a mile and more of water front, is left in smoking, hideous ruins." As destructive as the fire was, the city of Baltimore quickly began to rebuild and recover.

Library of Congress, Prints & Photographs Division [LC-F8-44294]

Smoke and ruins from the great Baltimore fire of 1904

Answer the questions about the text.

1. List two features of narrative nonfiction that this text contains.

_____

_____

2. What information does the primary source quotation add to the text?

_____

_____

3. How did the photograph impact your understanding of the fire?

_____

_____

Name _____

**Read each passage below. Use context clues to figure out the
meaning of each adage or proverb in bold. Write the meaning of
each one in a complete sentence. Underline the context clues
that helped you understand the adage or proverb.**

1. **As clouds gather before a storm**, the first sparks of flame
   foreshadowed an unthinkable disaster in New York City.

   _____

   _____

2. In this factory, **advice when most needed was least heeded**. There
   had been other fires at the Triangle Factory. Experts had called
   for more safety measures. In 1909 union workers protested the
   conditions in a strike. Their suggestions were ignored.

   _____

   _____

3. The owners were not convicted of a crime, but public outrage did
   lead to reform. Workers organized, and political leaders took action.
   Many would say that the reforms were **better late than never**.

   _____

   _____

4. For the women who lost their lives, however, it was **too little
   too late**.

   _____

   _____

Name _____

A. Read each adjective in bold. Then circle the word with the suffix that changes the adjective to a noun. Underline the suffix.

1. **important**   importance   import

2. **evident**   evidential   evidence

3. **defiant**   definitely   defiance

4. **excellent**   excellence   excelled

B. Read each pair of sentences and identify the word in bold. Then complete the second sentence by writing the word in the box that is related to the word in bold.

importance	persistent	violence	fragrance
observant	conference	disappearance	occurrence

5. The programmers **persisted** until they found a solution. They were very

   _____.

6. City leaders proudly reported there were fewer **violent** incidents this year.

   The amount of _____ has decreased.

7. The noisy crows **disappeared** from the trees last week. The neighborhood is much

   quieter since their _____.

8. The food baking in the oven was deliciously **fragrant**. The _____

   made my mouth water!

9. Experts on the topic **conferred** for days to find a solution. In the end, their

   _____ was quite successful.

Name _____

A. Read the draft model. Use the questions that follow the draft to help you think about how to make the style and tone more objective.

Draft Model

Cars kept zooming through our neighborhood like mad and not stopping at the stop sign. It was crazy dangerous to cross the streets.

---

1. How could the sentences or information in the draft be rewritten to reflect a more formal style?

2. Which words and phrases in the draft should be replaced or left out to create a more objective tone?

3. Would changing the narrator's voice help make the draft more objective? If so, what words and phrases should be changed?

B. Now revise the draft by changing the style and tone of the piece to give it a more formal and objective voice.

_____

_____

_____

_____

_____

_____

_____

_____

_____

_____

Name _____

The student who wrote the paragraphs below used details from two different sources to answer the question: *Could the Great Chicago Fire of 1871 have been prevented from spreading as far as it did?*

The Great Chicago Fire quickly spread from a poor neighborhood on the far west side of the city all the way through the downtown area and up to the far northern part. But according to first-hand accounts, it didn't have to spread that far.

On the first night of the fire, James Hildreth helped prevent the fire from spreading south. He used explosives to blow up empty houses. When the houses were leveled, many volunteers doused the debris with water, which soon stopped the fire's spread south. As the fire spread farther north, he attempted to do the same thing. He tried to gather volunteers, but "the word 'powder' was a terror to them." People ran away from him, and he gave up.

In an 1871 article of *The Nation* magazine, Frederick Law Olmstead suggested that the building materials used in fancy stone-faced walls contributed to the fire's spread. "...plain brick walls or walls of brick ... resisted the fire much better than stone-faced walls ...."

If people had volunteered, or if more homes were built from brick, the Chicago Fire might have not spread as far.

Reread the passage. Follow the directions below.

1. How could the Chicago Fire been prevented from spreading so far? **Circle** the clear reasons that provide evidence for the claim.

2. What style and tone were used in this writing sample? **Draw a box** around words that demonstrate the style and tone.

3. Could the fire have been prevented? **Underline** the sentence that introduces the claim.

4. **Write** an adverb on the line.

_____

Name _____

protein	correspond	saturated	extract
resilient	foliage	hypothesis	alternative

Finish each sentence using the vocabulary word provided.

1. **(foliage)** We went for a walk in the forest _____
_____.

2. **(saturated)** After the river flooded, _____
_____.

3. **(resilient)** The weeds in his yard _____
_____.

4. **(alternative)** If you don't want to explore the caves with us, _____
_____.

5. **(hypothesis)** The biology student _____
_____.

6. **(protein)** In order to be healthy, _____
_____.

7. **(extract)** The miners are trying _____
_____.

8. **(correspond)** Please check to make sure _____
_____.

Name _____

Read the selection. Complete the main idea and key details graphic organizer.

Main Idea

Detail

Detail

Detail

Name _____

Read the passage. Use the summarize strategy to check your understanding of key ideas.

Researching the Ocean's Secrets

9	Scientists didn't know much about deep-sea life until Jacques
16	Cousteau's inventions changed everything. Cousteau, a Frenchman,
30	wanted to dive deep below the surface of the sea. Skin divers had to
44	swim near the surface. They had no way to carry air with them. Cousteau
54	invented a portable breathing apparatus and an underwater camera. Those
67	inventions made it possible to explore the ocean and film the wonders of
	the sea.

69	**Goggles, Cameras, and Scuba Diving**
74	Goggles were not common diving gear in the 1930s. Free-swimming
84	divers usually swam without anything to cover their eyes. Cousteau tried
95	some goggles and was amazed at what he saw. His love for diving grew
109	even more. Cousteau was excited to share his discovery with the world,
121	but his camera would not work in water. So he figured out how to make it
137	waterproof. With goggles and an underwater camera, Cousteau was set to
148	make history.
150	Still, Cousteau wanted to dive deeper than was possible without an
161	air supply. He envied the freedom of the fish. However, there was no
174	equipment that allowed divers to breathe without hoses or tubes attached
185	to an air supply above the surface. Those lines fastened divers to a vessel
199	that carried their bulky air-supply equipment. In 1943 Cousteau and
209	Emile Gagnan invented a self-contained underwater breathing system.
217	They called the device the Aqua-Lung. This gear ushered in a new era in
231	underwater exploration. The equipment offered a way for divers to get air
243	under water without being connected to an air source above.
253	The new gear became known as Self-Contained Underwater Breathing
262	Apparatus, or SCUBA. The breathing apparatus fed air to divers at the
274	same pressure as the water around them. It allowed divers to spend more
287	time below. Scuba gear changed the way Cousteau and others explored
298	the oceans.

Name _____

From the Sea to TV

Cousteau's breathing machine and goggles allowed him to explore the depths of the sea. He needed a vessel, a boat of just the right size from which he could dive. In 1950 Cousteau acquired a small ship named *Calypso*. She was sturdy and built so she could go in and out of shallow coral reefs. *Calypso* was perfect for both exploring and filming Cousteau's underwater adventures.

Cousteau outfitted *Calypso* as a laboratory from which he could make dives. *Calypso*'s workspace carried underwater cameras and diving gear. A shark cage was lashed to the deck. An underwater observation room known as "*Calypso*'s false nose" was added to the vessel. The nose chamber was a large enough space for two of the crew to film under water. Cousteau wanted to share what he and his crew saw below.

Cousteau began recording his explorations. First, he used black-and-white film and later, color. *National Geographic* magazine noticed Cousteau's color pictures and invited him to work with them. They started filming his underwater adventures for television. Cousteau's films soon played on televisions across America on a weekly basis. His program became so popular that it ran for nine years. Cousteau narrated the shows himself, describing his discoveries with his engaging French accent.

Cousteau thought of his films as nature adventures. He was a scientist who had a sense of wonder about everything he did. He loved to explore unknown waters. Cousteau explored sea life with a sense of awe and shared that with his TV viewers.

Cousteau also brought attention to marine conservation, so that ocean life would be preserved instead of harmed. He founded the Cousteau Society in 1974. Cousteau brought the beauty and marvel of underwater life into people's homes. He inspired the world by sharing his love of the sea.

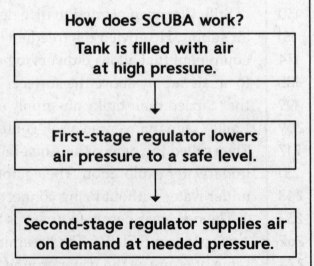

How does SCUBA work?

Tank is filled with air at high pressure.

↓

First-stage regulator lowers air pressure to a safe level.

↓

Second-stage regulator supplies air on demand at needed pressure.

Name _____

A. Reread the passage and answer the questions.

1. What is the main idea of the first paragraph? Which two details in the paragraph support the main idea?

_____

_____

_____

2. Give two key details in the second paragraph.

_____

_____

_____

3. What is the main idea of the second paragraph?

_____

_____

4. Look at the second paragraph under the heading "From the Sea to TV." Write one key detail and the main idea of that paragraph.

_____

_____

_____

_____

B. Work with a partner. Read the passage aloud. Pay attention to accuracy. Stop after one minute. Fill out the chart.

	Words Read	–	Number of Errors	=	Words Correct Score
First Read		–		=	
Second Read		–		=	

Name _____

Jane Goodall: Chimpanzee Expert

Interested in animals from a young age, Jane Goodall left England in 1960 and went to Gombe, Tanzania, in Africa. There, she began her lifelong study of chimpanzees. Unlike other scientists, Goodall took a very personal approach to her research. She gave the chimpanzees names instead of numbers. Goodall made many new discoveries about chimpanzees, including the fact that they are omnivores. In other words, they eat other animals as well as plants. In 1986 Goodall published her book *Chimpanzees of Gombe: Patterns of Behavior*. Today, Goodall travels 300 days a year. She educates others worldwide about wildlife conservation.

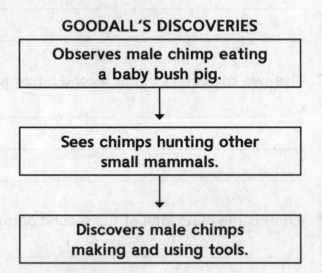

GOODALL'S DISCOVERIES

Observes male chimp eating a baby bush pig.

↓

Sees chimps hunting other small mammals.

↓

Discovers male chimps making and using tools.

Answer the questions about the text.

1. What technical term is included in this expository text? What does it mean?

   _____

   _____

2. Which step in the flow chart provides information that is different from the other two steps?

   _____

   _____

3. What can you conclude about Goodall's commitment to wildlife?

   _____

   _____

Name _____

Read each passage. Underline the context clues that help you figure out the meaning of each word in bold. Then answer the question below the passage.

1. **Goggles** were not common diving gear in the 1930s. Free-swimming divers usually swam without anything to cover their eyes.

   On what part of your body would you wear **goggles**? _____

2. In 1943 Cousteau and Emile Gagnan invented a self-contained underwater breathing system. They called the **device** the Aqua-Lung. This gear ushered in a new era in underwater exploration.

   What is an example of a **device** you might find in a kitchen? _____

3. He needed a **vessel**, a boat of just the right size from which he could dive. In 1950 Cousteau acquired a small ship named *Calypso*.

   What kind of **vessel** might you use on a small lake? _____

4. Cousteau outfitted *Calypso* as a **laboratory** from which he could make dives. *Calypso*'s workspace carried underwater cameras and diving gear.

   What happens in a **laboratory**? _____

5. An underwater observation room known as "*Calypso*'s false nose" was added to the vessel. The nose **chamber** was a large enough space for two of the crew to film under water.

   Instead of in a big theater, where do you think **chamber** music

   is usually played? _____

6. Cousteau also brought attention to marine **conservation**, so that ocean life would be preserved instead of harmed.

   What could help **conservation** of the oceans? _____

Name _____

technology	physician	heroism	geologist	politician
ecologist	apology	mythology	specialist	feminism
novelist	biologist	technician	patriotism	tourist

A. Read the words in the box. Sort the words by their Greek suffixes. Write each word in the correct column below.

-ician	*-logy*	*-ologist*	*-ist*	*-ism*
_____	_____	_____	_____	_____
_____	_____	_____	_____	_____
_____	_____	_____	_____	_____

Greek Suffixes

- *-ician* means "a specialist in"
- *-crat* and *-cracy* mean "rule"
- *-logy* and *-ologist* mean "science of" and "scientist"
- *-phobia* means "an abnormal fear"
- *-ist* means "one who practices"

B. Find the word in each row that matches the clue in bold. Write the word on the line and underline its suffix. Use the meanings of the Greek suffixes to help you.

1. **fear of water**   aquaphobia   anthropology   _____

2. **ruled by the people**   chemist   democracy   _____

3. **a specialist in music**   musical   musician   _____

4. **science of the heart**   cardiologist   cardiology   _____

Name _____

A. Read the draft model. Use the questions that follow the draft to help you think about using sequence to order steps in a process to help readers understand how and why something was done.

Draft Model

To make a goldfish home, you need a bowl or tank, purified water, and special gravel. Rinse the tank with some purified water. Clean the gravel with purified water. Put the gravel in the tank. Fill the tank with more purified water.

---

1. What word or phrase could you add to signal the first step in making a goldfish home?

2. What words or phrases could you use to signal the second and third steps in the process?

3. What word or phrase can you use to signal the last step in the process?

B. Now revise the draft by adding words and phrases that will help the reader understand the sequence of steps involved in setting up a goldfish home.

_____

_____

_____

_____

_____

_____

_____

_____

Name _____

The student who wrote the paragraphs below used details from two different sources to answer the question: *How has Hazel Barton used the scientific method to learn more about microbes?*

By the time Hazel Barton turned 14, she had an interest in microbiology. Over the years, she has combined her interests in microbiology and caving to explore the world's oldest forms of life on earth—single-cell organisms called microbes. To help her make new discoveries, she has used the scientific method.

First, Hazel observed microbes that live in dark caves with no sunlight and little food. Then she asked a question: "How do cave microbes adapt to such harsh conditions and manage to survive?"

Next, Hazel made a hypothesis that the microbes "create a community that works together to stay alive." Through initial testing, Hazel found five hundred species were good at making a living. Some organisms took energy from the air; some took energy from the rock; and some took energy from the soil. So she concluded that as a group, this community of microbes gets its energy from multiple sources.

Then Hazel had another question: How do the organisms work together? Hazel is still testing her hypothesis. Then she will have more conclusions to make and questions to ask.

Reread the passage. Follow the directions below.

1. What is the sequence of the steps in the scientific method? **Circle** the phrases that show evidence of a logical order.

2. **Draw a box** around a sentence that shows concrete details to support the topic.

3. **Underline** the sentence that shows the topic of this writing sample.

4. **Write** a negative word on the line.

_____

Name _____

exquisite   intrinsic   meticulously   excavation

bedrock   intriguing   methodical   embark

Use each pair of vocabulary words in a single sentence.

1. excavation, intriguing

_____

_____

_____

2. meticulously, bedrock

_____

_____

_____

3. methodical, intrinsic

_____

_____

_____

4. exquisite, embark

_____

_____

_____

Name _____

Read the selection. Complete the sequence graphic organizer.

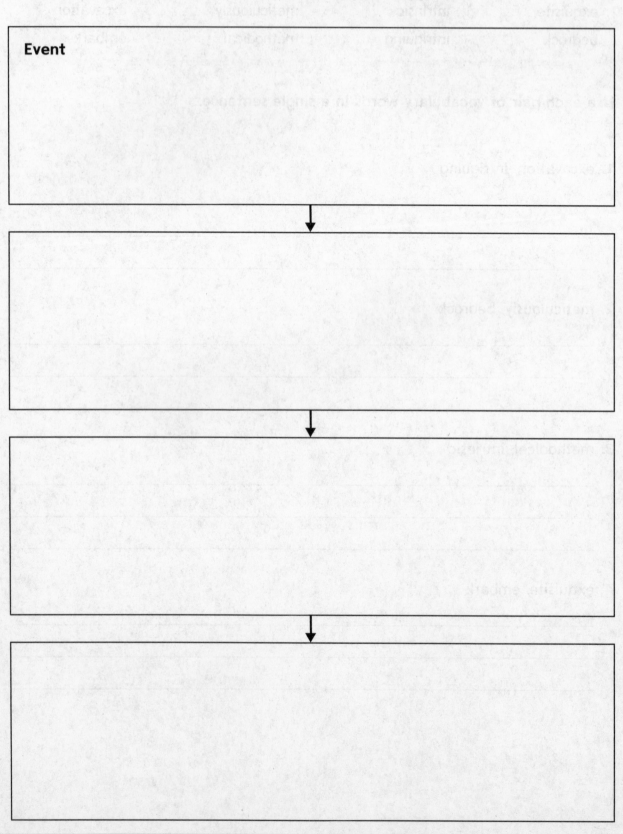

Name

Read the passage. Use the summarize strategy to restate the most important points.

Ancient Threads Reveal Early Weavers

13	From deep in a mountain cave in Peru, South America, ancient bits of cloth have given scientists a peek into the lives of the people who made
27	them. But when did they live? A new way of finding an object's age now
42	proves how old the cloth is. Scientists now know they are learning about a
56	culture that is at least 12,000 years old.

A New Kind of Test

64	
69	For many years, archaeologists did not have a good way to tell how
82	old their finds were. They could only compare objects found in the
94	same place and guess that they were from the same time period. Then
107	in 1947 a scientist named Willard Libby was trying to find out the age of
122	fossils for a paleontology study. Libby began thinking about a way to get
135	a more precise age. Libby came up with a theory based on the scientific
149	fact that living plants absorb a small amount of carbon-14. The amount of
162	carbon-14 decreases over time. Using logic, Libby inferred that he could
173	tell how long plants had been dead by measuring how much carbon-14
185	was left in them. He called this process "carbon dating." Thanks to Libby,
198	scientists can be more certain of the age of their discoveries.
209	In the 1980s, archaeologists first found signs that humans had lived
220	inside the cave in Peru. They used carbon dating to find the age of bone
235	and charcoal pieces found in the cave. Those objects all proved to be
248	around 12,000 years old. This proof was important. The information told
259	them that humans had visited the mountains near Peru soon after the last
272	glacier period ended around 12,500 years ago.

Name _____

More Advanced Dating

Archaeologists also found bits of rope and woven thread inside the cave in Peru. They found finely woven bits of fabric and bundles of plant material useful for weaving. From this find, archaeologists could tell that an advanced people had visited the cave. They did not know how old the samples were, however. Scientists knew humans had disturbed the cave at some time. No one knew when. So no one could say for sure if the bits of cloth had been left behind 100 years ago or 12,000 years ago.

The small pieces of cloth had not been tested with the other cave samples for a reason. Until lately, carbon testing was not reliable with small fragments. Finally, in 2011 a more advanced method of carbon dating was used on the bits of fabric. This technique can tell the age of even one hair. Archaeologists learned at last that the bits of fabric were also 12,000 years old. Now the scientists knew that prehistoric people had made them.

Guitarrero Cave is located in Peru in South America. Fibers found in the cave were left behind about 12,000 years ago.

After learning how old the fabric samples were, scientists were able to learn more about who visited the cave. Early researchers thought that humans had gone into the mountains to search for food. Hunters would likely have been men. From what is known about other cultures, scientists believe that women would have been the ones to weave the fabric. This suggests that women must also have gone into the mountains and must have stayed long enough to weave fabric. Perhaps the men hunted while the women made cloth and rope in the cave.

The latest ways of dating artifacts have led scientists to fresh understandings of ancient times. Carbon dating has given scientists a way to peer into the past—sort of like having a telescope on long ago. By finding out when something was made, scientists can discover more about the time before history was written.

Name_____

A. Reread the passage and answer the questions.

1. Look at the first paragraph under "A New Kind of Test." List the sequence of events that led to Willard Libby's carbon-dating process. What signal words help you follow the sequence?

_____

_____

_____

2. About how long after Libby developed the idea of carbon dating did scientists find signs of humans inside the cave? How do you know?

_____

_____

_____

_____

3. List the sequence of the steps that archaeologists took to learn about the people who lived in the mountain cave in Peru.

_____

_____

_____

_____

B. Work with a partner. Read the passage aloud. Pay attention to phrasing and rate. Stop after one minute. Fill out the chart.

	Words Read	–	Number of Errors	=	Words Correct Score
First Read		–		=	
Second Read		–		=	

Name _____

The Niaux Cave: Gallery of Prehistoric Art

The Niaux Cave, located in the Pyrenees Mountains in southern France, is famous for its prehistoric wall paintings. The cave entrance is set high on the side of a mountain. Scientists believe that because this landscape created a warm climate, the caves sheltered both animals and humans at the end of the last Ice Age. In 1906 a series of wall drawings of three bison, a horse, and a weasel were discovered in the main hall of Niaux Cave. In 1971 the first group of scientists studied the paintings. A process called radiocarbon dating was used to identify the age of the artwork. This process tested the charcoal used to create the paintings and confirmed that they were at least 14,000 years old.

CAROLUS/Pixtal/agefotostock

A prehistoric wall painting from the Niaux Cave in France

Answer the questions about the text.

1. List two features of expository text that this text contains.

   _____

   _____

2. What activity is described over a range of time?

   _____

   _____

3. What idea from the text does the photograph help you to visualize?

   _____

   _____

Name _____

A. Read each passage. Look at the meanings of the word parts. Then write a definition for the word in bold.

1. For many years, **archaeologists** did not have a good way to tell how old their finds were.

   archaeo = ancient, old; *logos* = study

   _____

2. Then in 1947 a scientist named Willard Libby was trying to find out the age of fossils for a **paleontology** study.

   paleo = prehistoric; *logos* = study

   _____

3. Finally, in 2011 a more advanced method of carbon dating was used on the bits of fabric. This **technique** can tell the age of even one hair.

   tech = skill

   _____

4. Carbon dating has given scientists a way to peer into the past— sort of like having a **telescope** on long ago.

   tele = far; *scope* = see

   _____

B. Write another word that has each of the following roots. Use a dictionary if necessary.

1. *tele* _____

2. *tech* _____

3. *ology* _____

Name _____

A. Complete the word equation by adding a prefix to each root word. Write the new word on the line.

1. im + patiently = _____

2. ac + commodate = _____

3. il + logical = _____

4. ar + rest = _____

5. ac + company = _____

6. im + migration = _____

B. Complete each sentence using the clue in parentheses.
Choose the correct absorbed form of the prefix from the box and add it to the root word in the clue. Write the word on the line.

Original Prefix and Meaning	Absorbed Forms
ad- means "to" or "toward"	*ac-, ar-, at-*
in- means "not" or "the opposite of"	*im-, ir-, il-*

7. The pieces of paper were _____ sizes. (not regular)

8. The driver made an _____ turn and caused an accident. (the opposite of legal)

9. I wanted to _____ my friend to the meeting after school. (to go with as company)

10. My pet dog is a very _____ puppy! (not mature)

Name _____

A. Read the draft model. Use the questions that follow the draft to help you think about how to choose time-order words to show the sequence of steps in a process.

Draft Model

    Marsha wanted to paint her desk. She prepared the area by putting down newspaper. She sanded the desk. She cleaned the surfaces gently. She let the desk dry. She started painting.

1. What time-order word or phrase could you use to show the first thing Marsha did to prepare the area for painting her desk?

2. What time-order words and phrases could you use to clarify the order of the next three steps Marsha took to prepare the desk for painting?

3. What time-order word or phrase could you add to identify the last thing Marsha did in this paragraph?

B. Now revise the draft by adding time-order words and phrases that will help readers better understand the order of steps in the process described.

_____

_____

_____

_____

_____

_____

Name _____

The student who wrote the paragraphs below used details from two different sources to respond to the prompt. *In "The Mystery of the Missing Sandals," Scott figures out who stole King Tut's golden sandals.* Pharaoh's Boat *tells about the restoration of an ancient Egyptian boat, but it also tells about a mystery. Explain how the mystery in* Pharaoh's Boat *was solved.*

When workers removed rubble next to Pharaoh's pyramid, they found that one boundary wall was 5 meters closer to the base of the pyramid than the other walls. They did not know why Egyptians would have done this, as they were usually meticulous in their measurements. Then Egyptologist Kamel el Mallakh figured that boat pits could be found behind the wall. After workers carefully uncovered the boat pits, Ahmed Youssef Moustafa was chosen to restore and rebuild the ancient ship.

Next, Ahmed researched ship-building methods and built scale models of the ship. He was stumped, however, because the ship-building methods he had studied didn't match up with the pieces that were found in the boat pit. Finally, he solved the mystery. He realized that the ancient Egyptians built the boat's frame after its shape had been created—an "ancient Egyptian shipbuilding secret."

Anytime archaeologists and restorers work to uncover the past, they are solving mysteries.

Reread the passage. Follow the directions below.

1. **Circle** the sentence that introduces the topic.

2. **Draw a box** around time-order words that describe the sequence of events.

3. **Underline** specific details and facts that support the topic.

4. **Write** a preposition and prepositional phrase on the line.

_____

_____

Name _____

incentive   horizons   recreation   unfettered

Finish each sentence using the vocabulary word provided.

1. **(unfettered)** I let my dog out of its cage _____

_____.

2. **(incentive)** My mother said she would take me to the movies _____

_____.

3. **(recreation)** Swimming at the local pool _____

_____.

4. **(horizons)** Learning how to speak a new language _____

_____.

Name _____

Read the selection. Complete the theme graphic organizer.

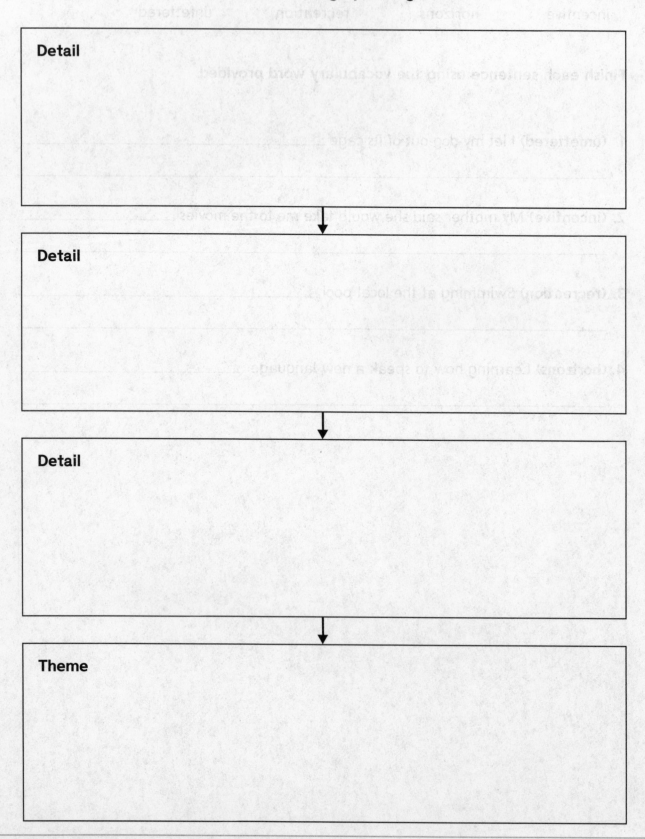

Detail

↓

Detail

↓

Detail

↓

Theme

Name _____

Read the passage. Check your understanding by asking yourself what the theme, or message, of the poem is.

Ode to Mr. Lincoln

	I watch as you sit on your marble chair,
9	I see your marble arms and hands, solid and firm
19	As the earth itself, and I think to myself those hands
30	Once held a whole country together. I think to myself
40	Those hands once held the future of democracy
48	As gently as morning light falls on a field of battle.
59	How could one man not bend under that burden?
68	You saw to it that people were free,
76	No matter their color or race or creed,
84	No matter what songs they sang.
90	You saw to it that all of your people had choices.
101	You followed the path you chose for yourself
109	As surely as the stars follow their paths across the sky.
120	The worries of your life are behind you, Mr. Lincoln,
130	Though once they lay heavy on your heart—
138	As weighty as mountains of stone on the horizon,
147	As numerous as snowflakes covering a burial ground.
155	The union has lasted far beyond four score and seven years,
166	but you can rest till time and tide are done
176	and let your thoughts wander wherever they will.

Photodisc/Punchstock

Name _____

A. Reread the passage and answer the questions.

1. What national monument is the poet referring to in the first two
   lines of the poem?

   _____

2. What lines describe Lincoln's accomplishments?

   _____

   _____

   _____

3. What does the phrase "The worries of your life are behind
   you" mean?

   _____

   _____

4. What theme, or message, about Lincoln does the poet convey to
   the reader?

   _____

   _____

**B. Work with a partner. Read the passage aloud. Pay attention to
expression and phrasing. Stop after one minute. Fill out the chart.**

	Words Read	–	Number of Errors	=	Words Correct Score
First Read		–		=	
Second Read		–		=	

Name _____

To an Artist

The city is bustling, noisy, and bright
With trucks, cars, and taxicabs, both day and night,
And with people so anxious to get here or there,
As they text on their cell phones and fuss with their hair.
On they go, pounding the pavement and street.
On they go, wearing their shoes off their feet.
At a corner an artist stands, paintbrush in hand,
A statue of silence observing the land.
Like a wizard, he captures a moment—Look! There!
Beauty on canvas; most pass, unaware.

Answer the questions about the text.

1. How do you know that this text is a lyric poem?

_____

_____

_____

_____

2. How do you know this text is also an ode?

_____

_____

3. What repetition can you find in the text?

_____

4. Choose one powerful image from the text. What message do you
think the poet tries to communicate with that image?

_____

_____

Name _____

Repetition is the repeating of a word or phrase. Poets use repetition to emphasize an idea and to give the poem rhythm.

Imagery is the use of words to create a vivid picture in the reader's mind.

Read the lines of the ode below. Then answer the questions.

Ode to Mr. Lincoln

I watch as you sit on your marble chair,
I see your marble arms and hands, solid and firm
As the earth itself, and I think to myself those hands
Once held a whole country together. I think to myself
Those hands once held the future of democracy
As gently as morning light falls on a field of battle.
How could one man not bend under that burden?

1. Find an example of repetition in the poem. Write it below.

   _____

2. Find two examples of imagery in the poem. Write them below.

   _____

   _____

3. How do the repetition and imagery affect the poem?

   _____

   _____

   _____

4. Write a short poem about someone you admire that includes repetition and imagery.

   _____

   _____

   _____

   _____

Name _____

**Read each passage and pay special attention to the hyperbole
in bold. Then decide whether the statement below the passage
expresses the true meaning of the hyperbole. If it does not, write
what you think the words in bold are meant to communicate.**

1. I see your marble arms and hands, **solid and firm**
   As the earth itself, and I think to myself those hands
   Once held a whole country together.

   Because they are marble, the statue's hands are actually as solid
   and firm as the earth.

   ☐ True   ☐ False

   _____

   _____

2. You followed the path you chose for yourself
   As surely as the stars follow their paths across the sky.

   Abraham Lincoln was extremely sure and steady in his beliefs
   and actions.

   ☐ True   ☐ False

   _____

   _____

3. The worries of your life are behind you, Mr. Lincoln,
   Though once they lay heavy on your heart—
   As weighty as mountains of stone on the horizon,
   As numerous as snowflakes covering a burial ground.

   Abraham Lincoln had millions of worries that weighed many tons.

   ☐ True   ☐ False

   _____

   _____

Name _____

Word from Mythology	Meaning
Ceres	Roman goddess of grain
Chaos	Greek goddess; formless gap between heaven and earth
Flora	Roman goddess of flowers
Iris	Greek goddess of the rainbow
Mercury	Roman messenger of the gods
Titans	Greek gods who were giants
Sol	Roman god of the sun
Psyche	Greek character who represents the human soul

Read each sentence below. Use the chart to underline the word that comes from one of the Greek or Roman names. Then circle the part of the word that it shares with the name from mythology.

1. We used special glasses to view the solar eclipse.

2. He gave his mother a floral bouquet on her birthday.

3. The powerful hurricane threw the town into chaos.

4. What is your sister's favorite breakfast cereal?

5. A titanic wave washed onto the deserted shore.

6. During the science experiment, the teacher poured mercury into the glass.

7. I want to study psychology so I can understand the way people think.

8. We picked a colorful iris from the garden.

Name_____

A. Read the draft model. Use the questions that follow the draft to help you choose words with connotations that accurately express the speaker's feelings.

Draft Model

I like to look at clouds as they move across the sky. They look like a good place to lie down and take a nap or read a book.

---

1. Why do the clouds look like a good place to lie down and take a nap? What words make you think of a relaxing place?

2. How might it feel to lie down on the clouds? What words will best convey how the speaker feels about lying in the clouds?

3. How would you describe time passed in the clouds? What words best convey the sort of experience the speaker might have on a cloud?

B. Now revise the draft by adding descriptive words with connotations that accurately and clearly express the speaker's feelings.

_____

_____

_____

_____

_____

_____

_____

Name _____

The student who wrote the poem below used details from two different sources to respond to the prompt: *Write a lyric poem about the importance of taking a break—to rest, to think, or to dream.*

On most days I'm busy
with school, chores, and studies,
and then there's basketball practice
and time with my buddies.

And I like being busy.
I'm on top of my game.
But too much "busy"
and I feel pretty lame.

That's when I stop—
to feel rested; restored.
How do I do it?
I get really bored.

'Cause I love when there's
absolutely nothing to do.
My head sprouts ideas
from out of the blue!

I have time to see
with my mind's open eye
how to let quiet thoughts in
and let busy thoughts lie.

So when I feel myself sprinting
up an impossible hill,
I stop.
I get bored.
And I take time to chill.

Reread the passage. Follow the directions below.

1. **Circle** an example of figurative language.

2. How does the narrator of the poem feel about being bored? **Draw a box** around words that show the narrator's feelings.

3. How does the author use sensory language? **Underline** an example.

4. **Write** an example of how two sentences might have been combined to avoid repetition.

_____

_____